PUBLISHED IN JUNE 1993

D1796185

FOULSHAM'S
ORIGINAL MOORE'S
ALMANACK

1697 *THE ORIGINAL COPYRIGHT EDITION* **1994**

1994: Year of Recovery

I have christened 1994 the Year of Recovery because, although the world will still be in the grip of uncertainty and instability, the pace of change will now slow down, allowing people and governments to catch up with the disintegration which began in 1987-8. The simple reason is that the Uranus-Neptune conjunction, which represents idealism and vision, but confusion and muddle in practical affairs, is now at an end. It was this conjunction which dissolved the iron curtain, bringing an end to the rigid political forms of Eastern Europe. The two planets maintain their conjunction until the end of 1995, but the exact contact has now passed and we can now begin to talk about reconstruction.

However, if we look ahead, it will be the end of the 1990s before we can truly have any idea of what the new 'world order' is to be. In 1996-7 the planetary cyclical index, the most accurate measure of instability, reaches its trough, indicating that the uncertainty of Uranus-Neptune will be extended until then. In addition, the Sunspot cycle, which measures a series of economic and cultural cycles, reaches a trough, confirming that these years will bring an international turning point. Final confirmation is added by the fact that Uranus, Neptune and Pluto will all be moving into new signs between then and the end of the century.

© **1993 by W. FOULSHAM & CO. LTD.** Tel. **SLOUGH (0753) 526769**
Printed in England by Benham & Co, Colchester

The only conclusion is that most governments will still be stumbling in the dark, and that questions such as the pace of European union and relations between the former communist and capitalist worlds will still be unanswered. Relations between the Islamic and European worlds will also still be confused and the potential cause of massive conflict.

The world economy will begin under very shaky influences. The London stock exchange could fall by as much as 20% in the weeks following January 15th. A difficult Jupiter-Mars square on February 25th represents the worst point on economic decline. However, after then the global pressures are generally supportive, signified by the extended trine aspect between Jupiter and Saturn. This indicates that, after January, economic confidence will grow until the end of the year. Within this overall pattern a low point can be expected around June 1st. A high point can be expected over the last half of March. After the eclipse on November 18th economic confidence is likely to be in a free fall until the end of the year. At the end of December a rare Mars-Jupiter-Saturn aspect indicates another economic trough, leading into 1995. In the US there are strong indications of a returning economic boom, although this could be knocked off course at the end of the year. The UK will experience economic recovery in the latter part of the year, although it will be less marked than in the US. Germany on the other hand, shows no signs of emerging from economic troubles.

The Uranus-Neptune conjunction will be encouraging the spread of religions and ideologies, and will encourage schisms and splits between groups who each imagine that they have the absolute monopoly of the truth. Increasingly, it will also dissolve the boundaries between science and religion, as it becomes clear that the distinctions between consciousness and matter are much closer than was once believed.

In the World Horoscope Aries is rising. Jupiter is the primary ruler and Mars is the secondary ruler. This is an extraordinary potent indicator of powerful and controlled feelings and a belief that anything is possible. The only risk is that, due to Mars' presence, it will be imagined that war can be used to pursue ideals which in themselves may be perfectly just. It will be necessary for those in authority to consciously develop the qualities of Saturn, namely excessive caution.

The Kabbalistic analysis of 1994 (i.e. 1+9+9+4 =23=2+3=5) is represented by the Tarot trump, the Hierophant, or High Priest. This indicates that the year will be dominated by moral questions, perhaps a backlash against current norms.

Old Moore extends his wish to all readers for a peaceful and prosperous year ahead.

Old Moore, December 1992

A Startling Memory Feat That You Can Do

How I learned the secret in one evening. It has helped me every day.

WHEN my old friend Richard Faulkner invited me to a dinner party at his house, I little thought it would be the direct means of doubling my salary in less than two years.

Towards the end of the evening things began to drag a bit as they often do at parties. Finally someone suggested the old idea of having everyone do a 'party-piece'.

When it came to Peter Brown's turn, he said he had a simple 'trick' which he hoped we would like. First he asked to be blindfolded. Then he asked someone to shuffle a deck of cards and call them out in order. Still blindfolded he instantly named the cards in their order backwards and forwards without making a single mistake.

You may well imagine our amazement at Peter's remarkable memory feat.

On the way home that evening I asked Peter Brown how it was done. He said there was really nothing to it — simply a memory feat. Anyone could develop a good memory, he said, by following a few simple rules. And then he told me exactly how to do it.

What Peter said I took to heart. In one evening I made remarkable strides towards improving my memory. In just a few days I learned to do exactly what he had done.

The most gratifying thing about the improvement of my memory was the remarkable way it helped me in business and in my social life. I discovered that my memory training had literally put a razor edge on my mind. My thinking had become clearer, quicker, keener.

Then I noticed a marked improvement in my writing and conversational powers. What's more my salary has increased dramatically.

These are only a few of the hundreds of ways I have profited by my trained memory. No longer do I suffer the frustration of meeting people I know and not being able to recall their names. The moment I see someone I have met before a name leaps into my mind. Now I find it easy to recall everything I read. I can now master a subject in considerably less time than before. Price lists, reports, quotations, data of all kinds. I can recall in detail almost at will. I rarely make a mistake.

What Peter told me that eventful evening was this: "Send for details of Dr. Furst's Memory Course." I did. That was my first step in learning to do all the remarkable things I have told you about. In fact, I was so impressed that I got permission to publish Dr.

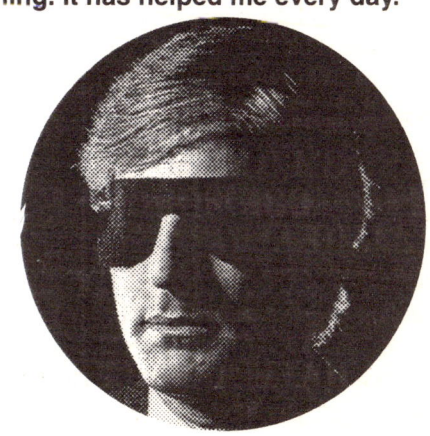

Furst's Course myself.

My advice to you now is don't wait another minute. Full details of Dr. Furst's remarkable Course are available free on request. Post the coupon today.

BOB HEAP

* * * * *

We, the publishers, have printed full details of Dr. Furst's unique memory training method in a free book entitled "Adventures in Memory". For your free copy simply post the coupon below (no stamp needed). Or write to: Memory and Concentration Studies (Dept. OMM53), FREEPOST 246, London WC1A 1BR.

WORLD AFFAIRS — A Prophetic View

THE WORLD PROPHETIC PREVIEW

In general 1994 is relatively free of dramatic planetary alignments, and we can now begin to look back on the period from 1989 to 1992 as one of those dramatic periods of history when change moves so fast that people, nations and governments lose their bearings, much like 1965-1969. However, the period of uncertainty is not over and we are not yet in a position to look back and see where it has been leading us. Although economic conditions will improve, recession will still be with us, and although the chances of war are not as great as they were in 1993, great caution is still required.

WAR AND PEACE

There are crisis spots in the world which have a momentum of their own, such as the Gulf, and these continue without igniting wider conflict. However, the Balkans war is still in danger of spreading, especially at the two most violent points of the year; mid-January and late November to early December. Most people have forgotten that in the nineteenth century the Balkans was the scene of inter-power rivalry between Russia and the Slavic world on the one hand, and the west on the other. The Balkans conflict has the capacity to draw in Romania, Bulgaria, the Ukraine, Russia, Turkey and Greece. A likely flashpoint for Greece would be the beginning of June and for Turkey mid-February and mid-October. Bearing in mind that these countries also have problems with each other (and in the case of Turkey with other neighbours), these are dates to watch in general for instability in these countries. However, it should be noted that, while astrological pressure on the Balkans continues until the end of 1995, the eclipse of November 18th, 1994, is the last of the series of profoundly disturbing astrological pressures to hit the area. Therefore, while this date brings serious problems for those wishing to contain the conflict, after this date the peacemakers will begin to regain the advantage.

THE UNITED KINGDOM AND CONSTITUTIONAL BATTLES

The eclipse of November 18th, also represents the last of the seriously threatening aspects to hit both the British Monarchy and Conservative Party. The Conservative Party can therefore expect to finally move out of the period of civil war which has afflicted it since 1989, and the first leadership challenge against Margaret Thatcher. Should any ambitious Parliamentarian wish to topple the party leader, there could be no better moment. The Queen will continue to experience unsettling transits in 1995, but of a considerably more moderate nature than those of 1990-3. Prince Charles will have passed all his powerful transits. Princess Diana, like the Queen, will find her last great test in the November eclipse. We may therefore expect that if there is to be a further Royal trauma, such as an announcement concerning the succession, or Charles and Diana's marriage, it should come in November. However, after then the Royal crisis should begin to become a thing of the past. If we look at the causes of the decline of Royal reputations in the early 90's, we can see that the key lies in the Royal Family's failure to perceive that the national mood had changed at the end of the 80's, and people were no longer prepared to see the Royals living it up while the people as a whole coped with recession. This was not inevitable; if the Queen had paid tax earlier, if Fergie and Diana had handled their marriage breakdowns with dignity, the crisis would have been considerably less traumatic. The lesson is that while certain astrological trends are predetermined, their exact consequences are not. Therefore, while the Queen is under stressful transits in 1994, she should seize the opportunity to make the Monarchy genuinely relevant. We are not talking about the spurious opening up of the sixties and seventies in which the television cameras were invited to view Royal privilege, but a serious tackling of the Monarchy's constitutional relationship role. Pressure will be kept up in the Labour Party which may finally democratise its constitution in June or July, and relaunch itself in September. Once the Labour Party challenges the status quo, questioning, for example, the hereditary control of the House of Lords, the Queen will have to bring her own role up to date. If she doesn't take such steps, the November eclipse could rebound on her very badly.

THE UNITED STATES
The United States of America declared their independence with a powerful conjunction of the Sun, Jupiter and Venus in Cancer. Two very helpful aspects are made to this conjunction in 1994, one a trine from Saturn, the other a trine from Jupiter. Individually these aspects would be very mild indicators of confidence and prosperity. Together they suggest that the US will be in an extremely buoyant mood and that there are excellent chances of an economic boom. Unfortunately there is no one single period when the planets are in a perfect alignment, but the strongest months are March, June and October. If the US is strong and confident, this also points to other conclusions. For example, a powerful foreign policy increases the chances of a low-level trade war. The time of the US Declaration of Independence is unknown, which means that there are a number of uncertainties in the horoscope for that event. However, given this flexibility, there is an extremely high chance in November either that the US will be drawn into a very bitter foreign war, or that there will be extremely serious inner-city riots, or an attack on a major politician.

CHINA
The horoscope for Communist China is due to experience extremely powerful transits in 1997. They are so strong that we can forecast that, even if there were to be some political disintegration, that year will see China's elevation to the status of a major world economic power. 1994 will see the continued emergence of a new leadership untouched by the revolutionary war, whose goal is to create an authoritarian capitalist state. We are unlikely to see dramatic news from China in 1994, for the opposition between transiting Saturn and the country's own Saturn indicates a period of solid, practical restructuring. The end of May is a sensitive period, when there could be some leadership changes, but the most important months are September and October. The first week of September brings the maximum chance of a complete transformation of the government, with the last of the Old Guard disappearing while new and younger faces appear in the lower levels of the regime.

JAPAN
Japan will enter a period of political instability at the end of the year. Although political corruption has become a feature of Japanese political life, the transits of November to December indicate something shocking even by existing standards. It would not be surprising to see the entire government replaced.

BILL CLINTON

Paul Conklin — Camera Press

There's no doubt about it. The psyche of the American people hasn't been so emotionally galvanized by a new president since the election of John F. Kennedy 33 years ago. Bill Clinton seems to represent the values, the goals, the beauty and naivite of the American dream in a way which makes him the perfect President for these times. Starting from the outermost planet in the chart, we see that Clinton is the first Pluto-in-Leo president, meaning that the younger generation is finally in power, the young king has truly ousted the old order. Clinton has his Sun and three other planets in Leo, the sign to do with the innocence of the child, the nobility of the king, and the special creativity of the human being which must be expressed with dignity in the running of the world. His Leo Sun is placed in the 11th house, which shows that he naturally finds his sense of meaning through group enterprise and service to the nation. The President enjoys the Leonine ability to dramatically express his beliefs and ideals, in a way which inspires others to seek the highest in themselves. The Sun-Jupiter-Uranus configuration gives the new leader an inventive and far-seeing mind and a broad philosophical outlook.

But Clinton has more than the legendary vision of fiery Leo. His earthy Taurus Moon gives him the practicality and hard-headedness necessary for playing such a difficult and powerful political role. Its position in the 8th house gives him plenty of economic savvy — he knows all about essential human needs, which governments must respect if success is to be assured. And this Taurean component, plus the indefatigability of his Saturn-Pluto conjunction, gives him enormous staying power and ambition. Clinton is not just the fresh-faced Mr Nice Guy but it doesn't hurt to have charismatic Libra rising with a Mars-Neptune-Venus conjunction swooning around his Ascendant, with Jupiter just a bit further on. Such a strong Libran emphasis gives tremendous idealism, desire for justice and harmony, easy popularity, and an innate awareness that respect for all viewpoints must be maintained. Here also is the source of Clinton's natural diplomacy, his love of music, and his appeal to women. Clinton works best in partnerships, and it is well known that Hilary is much more than an invisible power behind the throne. Librans are famous for their need to redress the balance, and we see this tendency in Clinton, especially in his desire to put more women into powerful political posts. This chart reveals a shrewd thinking, genuinely compassionate, and spiritually committed personality who, blessed with the common touch, can stay in tune with the people of America as well as remaining dedicated to the hard task that lies ahead of everyone.

The transits of 1993 and 1994 could not be much tougher for Clinton: the Saturn-Pluto square configures his Leo Sun in a stressful way, indicating that the American people will be waking up to the stringent sacrifices necessary to get their economy back on some sort of sane direction. In these recessionary times, Clinton's power is limited. If the weaknesses of his Libran Mars-Neptune dominate, he may discover that he is too susceptible to political pressure and he may fall prey to competing interests. He will depend strongly on his carefully chosen cabinet. Hopefully, together and with inspired team-work, they can help the new President devise a road map that helps take the country and him through this dangerous and difficult year of initiation.

Your 1994 Birthday

YOUR PERSONAL FORTUNE AND GUIDE

One of the following monthly readings is **PERSONAL TO YOU. Good days for Romance, Business, Finance, Travel and Social Affairs.** Each monthly forecast gives both your general and actual Birthday fortune for 1994 as well as

YOUR PLANETS, BIRTHSTONE AND YOUR LUCKY DAY

CAPRICORN BORN PEOPLE

Birthdays between December 22nd and January 20th inclusive. Your planet is Saturn. Birthstone, garnet. Lucky day, Saturday.

KEYNOTE FOR THE YEAR   Give credit where it is due at the start of the year and you will receive your kindness back ten-fold later. A good year for sorting out professional matters and for making general progress.

JANUARY   INFLUENCES: 1-2nd Concentrate on the job in hand and don't be side-tracked by details. 15-16th Help comes from some very unexpected directions at this time. 29-30th The practicalities of life demand most of your attention. OPPORTUNITIES: 9-10th You have a good ability now to break through any red-tape that exists in your working life. LIMITING INFLUENCES: 24-25th Arrangements have a habit of going wrong and this means that you will have to plan very carefully indeed at this stage.

FEBRUARY   INFLUENCES: 1-2nd Loving messages come your way and bring some surprising news with them. 14-15th The deeper and more intense side of Capricorn shows now so make certain you explain yourself carefully. 27-28th Despite the apparently difficult attitudes of others, you manage to get your message across intact. OPPORTUNITIES: 7-8th Make time for a sense of freedom and to please yourself a little. LIMITING INFLUENCES: 22-23rd A confusing time, and one in which others are doing very little to help.

MARCH   INFLUENCES: 1-2nd After a very promising start to the month, some quietness should be expected. 9-10th People reach a new understanding about the sort of person you are and what you want from life. 28-29th Not an ideal period for guessing things, so make certain about your facts in any given situation. OPPORTUNITIES: 6-7th Life leads you into some interesting paths at this time and you can take advantage of good fortune. LIMITING INFLUENCES: 20-21st No matter how optimistic you try to be, things still go wrong.

APRIL   INFLUENCES: 1-2nd A secretive period and one in which it is very difficult to get anyone else to spill the beans. 10-11th An ideal period for travelling or for making appointments that have been waiting for a while. 25-26th Restrictions come from a number of different directions. 30th Guard against minor infections or irritations. OPPORTUNITIES: 3-4th A secure spell, when it is possible to please yourself generally. LIMITING INFLUENCES: 17-18th Although you do all you can to understand others, the favour is not returned.

CAPRICORN BORN PEOPLE

MAY INFLUENCES: 3-4th Concentration is important in practical matters and there should be significant support from friends. 12-13th An unusual period though probably very productive and quite rewarding. 30-31st Most Capricorns will be showing great determination at this time and getting their own way. OPPORTUNITIES: 1-2nd Your true personality has the chance to shine out, much to the joy of those around you. LIMITING INFLUENCES: 18-19th Obstructions come suddenly and make life quite hard work.

JUNE INFLUENCES: 1-2nd A good start to the month and marking the start of an excellent time for travel and meetings of any sort. 12-13th In practical matters you need to get down to brass tacks just as quickly as you can. 27-28th A promising interlude and very good romantically speaking. OPPORTUNITIES: 24-25th Because you are so single-minded. very few people are likely to be ignoring you. LIMITING INFLUENCES: 14-15th Standard responses will not work at all well, so be flexible and original.

JULY INFLUENCES: 1-2nd Not such a promising beginning to July, perhaps because you are being a little hesitant. 19-20th There are some interesting people around and many of them could be of significant use to you at present. 25-26th Continual attention to detail could lead to unnecessary fatigue. OPPORTUNITIES: 21-22nd Now able to state your case carefully you can win favour with those around you. LIMITING INFLUENCES: 6-7th A stand-alone period when you look for support but may not receive it.

AUGUST INFLUENCES: 2-3rd Make time for necessary changes around your home. 15-16th Travel opportunities are good, an excellent time for taking a holiday. 22-23rd A fresh and invigorating period with plenty going your way. 29-30th You seem to have a particularly high profile in company. OPPORTUNITIES: 18-19th Security is on your mind and you can make life much more comfortable. LIMITING INFLUENCES: 4-6th Friends and relatives alike prove to be quite argumentative.

SEPTEMBER INFLUENCES: 4-5th Potentially a quiet period, though with positive undertones where you are willing to take note of them. 19-20th The real Capricorn is now on display, with practicality being the most important quality. 30th Avoid creeping about, the bigger and better you do things, the more you are being noticed. OPPORTUNITIES: 14-15th Without doubt the best part of the month to get yourself noticed. LIMITING INFLUENCES: 28-29th Some Capricorns are now far too quick to take offence.

OCTOBER INFLUENCES: 1-2nd Not a wonderful start to the month but here are some compliments about. 17-18th Misunderstandings abound and that means you should be very tactful. 29-30th People recognise your presence and power and are unwilling to cross swords with you. OPPORTUNITIES: 11-12th Look out for unusual but important possibilities on offer on both these days. LIMITING INFLUENCES: 25-27th Look out now because it is particularly difficult to conform to the expectations that others have of you.

NOVEMBER INFLUENCES: 4-5th Make bonfire night special, not only for yourself but for those who rely so much upon you. 15-16th Romance flourishes and you have the ability to move general obstacles that get in your way. 27-28th Look for new and interesting ways to make money, thanks to your practical approach. OPPORTUNITIES: 7-8th Not a time to be following conventions quite so much as you normally would, flexibility can bring great rewards. LIMITING INFLUENCES: 22-23rd Excessive tiredness could lead to some mistakes in professional matters.

DECEMBER INFLUENCES: 2-3rd Use your creative potential to the full and be bold when dealing with superiors. 12-13th Conforming to the expectations of those around you could be quite difficult. 21-22nd Take some extra rest in the final run-up to Christmas. OPPORTUNITIES: 5-6th Look out for a physical and mental peak that allows great progress. LIMITING INFLUENCES: 19-20th Quieter than of late, you may be too slow to register your protest if you feel others are being unfair with you.

AQUARIUS BORN PEOPLE

Birthdays between January 21st and February 19th inclusive. Your planet is Uranus. Birthstone, amethyst. Lucky day, Saturday.

KEYNOTE FOR THE YEAR   There are many unusual trends to be dealt with this year, though it is true to say that by far the majority of them work in your favour. A good year for consolidating gains and making changes.

JANUARY   INFLUENCES: 1-2nd A fairly dynamic start to the year, but don't take on more than you have to. 14-15th There could be a problem or two relating to rules and regulations. 28-29th Efforts are well worthwhile and now is a time to be bold in all your endeavours. OPPORTUNITIES: 11-12th Whatever you manage to do at this time, you tend to do it with flair. LIMITING INFLUENCES: 26-27 With a slight lack of confidence it is possible that others can easily divert you from the path you choose.

FEBRUARY   INFLUENCES: 1-2nd Start the month by being as creative as you can and by seeing where you can help others. 14-15th It isn't easy for others to understand what makes you tick, so explain yourself. 27-28th Those around you can be of great support if you are willing to rely on them. OPPORTUNITIES: 9-10th An unconventional approach to life works best and there are great gains to be made. LIMITING INFLUENCES: 24-25th Family members could be especially difficult to deal with.

MARCH   INFLUENCES: 3-4th Aquarius is deeper and more secretive now than would usually be the case. 15-16th. Try your hand at getting things done around the house, you could surprise yourself. 26-27th Imagination can be a great support to at a time when you are particularly creative in any case. OPPORTUNITIES: 9-10th A sunny period, and one in which it is easy to make others as happy as you are yourself. LIMITING INFLUENCES: 23-24th Make certain that you are speaking the absolute truth, it's important at present.

APRIL   INFLUENCES: 1-2nd You might be expecting a little too much of yourself at the beginning of the month, take time out to think. 15-16th Look for comfort and security in and around your own home. 24-25th You should find it possible to turn your mind and your hand to almost anything and can be of great help to loved-ones. OPPORTUNITIES: 5-6th Things you have been trying to do for a while now start to pay off. LIMITING INFLUENCES: 20-21st For once your objectivity goes right out of the window.

MAY   INFLUENCES: 4-5th It could be too easy so near the start of the month to put your foot in it when talking to relatives. 12-13th More quiet than usual, you do what you can to sort out one or two outstanding problems. 28-29th Get tedious jobs out of the way before you start efforts to have a good time. OPPORTUNITIES: 2-3rd The present position of the Moon makes you carefree and happy. LIMITING INFLUENCES 17-18th Don't tax yourself too much physically and leave time for personal choices.

JUNE INFLUENCES: 1-2nd Important decisions won't wait, so make up you mind as soon as you can. 10-11th The more you express yourself to others, the better the response you manage to get from them. 29-30th A time to specialise in the things that you are especially good at. Look out for sound assistance. OPPORTUNITIES: 26-27th Variety really does help now and breaks the mould of situations that are outdated. LIMITING INFLUENCES: 13-14th Too much concern for other people could be as bad as too little.

JULY   INFLUENCES: 2-3rd Utilise your communication skills and make the most of your general popularity. 14-15th An urge for personal freedom really makes you speak your mind at present. 29-30th A deeply romantic interlude comes along, so make the most of it at every opportunity. OPPORTUNITIES: 23-25th Most Aquarians are now in a more chatty frame of mind and you can talk your way in or out of practically anything. LIMITING INFLUENCES: 10-11th It might not be too easy to be totally objective, so be diplomatic.

AQUARIUS BORN PEOPLE

AUGUST   INFLUENCES: 2-3rd Friends can be critical and you may have to be especially tactful in your dealings with them. 14-15th Coincidences crop up, most of them turning to your advantage before very long. 27-28th Ideas come your way from a number of different directions and your natural talents are to the fore. OPPORTUNITIES: 20-21st People from the past crop up in your life again and bring new ideas. LIMITING INFLUENCE: 7-8th One or two small worries can be blown up out of all proportion.

SEPTEMBER   INFLUENCES: 1-2nd People seem determined to try your patience at every turn, so be diplomatic and patient. 14-15th. Finances should be stronger, so you should be able to splash out a little. 29-30th Irritations are about, but they are unlikely to divert you from your chosen path. OPPORTUNI-TIES: 16-17th Confidences bring some surprising news that can be turned to your advantage, both now and later. LIMITING INFLUENCES: 3-4th Life drives a hard bargain now and it would be all too easy to become over-tired.

OCTOBER   INFLUENCES: 1-2nd The month starts in a really practical way, and your efforts do not go without reward. 19-20th Practical matters demand your attention and new incentives crop up at every turn. 25th Excitement seems to be on the way, thanks to the intervention of other people. 31st End the month with a flourish and let others know what you are worth. OPPORTUNITIES: 13-14th Present gains come as a result of effort that you have put in previously. LIMITING INFLUENCES: 28-29th Confidence may be low.

NOVEMBER   INFLUENCES: 3-4th Quality hours to spend with your partner may be difficult to find, but do your best. 19-20th New excitement may be on the way, both in a practical and a personal way. 29-30th Easy ways to make money could turn out to be more difficult than you thought. OPPORTUNITIES: 9-10th This is the time for a physical and mental peak for most Aquarians. LIMITING INFLUENCES: 24-26th It's often hard for Aquarians to conform to expectations, and especially so now.

DECEMBER   INFLUENCES: 2-3rd Energy may be a little lacking but there is no shortage of ideas about. 14-15th Concentrate on one job for these two days and you may make unexpected gains. 25-26th An especially happy Christmas time, the more so because everyone around you is so willing to join in. OPPORTUNITIES: 7-8th Personalities abound and social possibilities go out through the roof. LIMIT-ING INFLUENCES: 21-23rd Financial pressure should not be allowed to divert your plans for more than a couple of days.

PISCES BORN PEOPLE

Birthdays between February 20th and March 20th inclusive. Your planet is Neptune. Birthstone, bloodstone. Lucky day, Thursday.

KEYNOTE FOR THE YEAR   Routines can be something of a chore at the beginning of the year, though with determination on your part these can easily be turned to your advantage. Personalities abound in your life

JANUARY   INFLUENCES: 1-2nd Make the start of the year special by doing what you really fancy and not so much of what you are told. 19-20th New responsibilities make you even keener to achieve success. 28-29th You should now feel yourself to be more in charge of your own destiny. OPPORTUNI-TIES: 15-16th Even casual conversations can have a positive outcome at this time. LIMITING INFLU-ENCES: 30-31st Not everyone is willing to listen to what you have to say and much patience on your part is necessary.

PISCES BORN PEOPLE

FEBRUARY   INFLUENCES: 2-3rd The start of the month is not dynamic, though useful all the same. 15-16th A more dynamic Piscean is now in evidence so be bold in all that you decide to do. 24-25th Keeping an open mind is not so easy, though essential if you want to make progress. OPPORTUNITIES: 12-13th Although you may not feel that you are moving forward now, the evidence begins to prove that you really are. LIMITING INFLUENCES: 26-27th A time to sit and take stock and not a dynamic interlude at all.

MARCH   INFLUENCES: 2-3rd Brings help and support from all sorts of unexpected directions. 14-15th Rivals come and go, though they can do little to dampen your enthusiasm. 29-30th Conventions do not appear to be too appealing now and you long to simply please yourself. OPPORTUNITIES: 11-12th Better fortune appears to be on offer, partly thanks to your own ability to apply yourself at present. LIMITING INFLUENCES: 26-27th Some pressure is felt, though of course you are not forced to respond to it.

APRIL   INFLUENCES: 1-2nd A start to the month that is full of energy and enterprise, though not everyone is willing to help out. 13-14th Conversation is stimulating and your love-life should be improving. 26-27th As the month draws to its close, be certain that you explain yourself as fully as you can. OPPORTUNITIES: 8-9th With energy and determination, practicalities are now sorted out in no time at all. LIMITING INFLUENCES: 22-23rd People may well fail to respond in the way that you are inclined to expect.

MAY   INFLUENCES: 1-2nd It's glorious May again and you should be able to greet the month with quite a smile. 12-13th No lack of willpower at present, though not everyone is exactly helpful. 26-27th Start new regimes now for a good chance of making them pay off. OPPORTUNITIES: 5-6th You simply charge through any sort of job at present without any real difficulty at all. LIMITING INFLUENCES: 19-20th Look for extra space to breath because you could feel hemmed in by circumstances at this time.

JUNE   INFLUENCES: 2-3rd A good time to communicate your needs and wants to people who are in a position to help you out. 9-10th Guard against misunderstandings that could well strike home in friendship circles. 26-27th A quiet interlude, though useful all the same. OPPORTUNITIES: 28-29th Confidence is not lacking and you can afford to back your hunches at this time. LIMITING INFLUENCES: 15-16th Stick to routines since this is not a period for taking too many chances or for pushing your luck.

JULY   INFLUENCES: 1-2nd Quite a dynamic start to the month, even if not everyone proves to be exactly helpful. 16-17th Go with the flow when it comes to doing the things you know to be essential. 29-30th Fulfilling all your obligations could be something of a drag at this time, but don't react too much. OPPORTUNITIES: 26-27th This period can be a feast of delights if you make the effort to keep your eyes open. LIMITING INFLUENCES: 13-14th Grab opportunities with both hands, but avoid tiring yourself.

AUGUST   INFLUENCES: 3-4th A little too tied down by routines, you feel the need of a break. 16-17th Offer as much support to others as you can manage to do. Alterations seem inevitable at this time. 27-28th Look for originality in everything and don't turn down chances. OPPORTUNITIES: 22-23rd Startling news could really change some important events in your life for the better. LIMITING INFLUENCES: 9-10th Faults and failings in others may only reflect the way that your own mind is working during this interlude.

SEPTEMBER   INFLUENCES: 1-2nd Things go well in a general sense, though you may want to slow life down just a little. 5-7th Confidence is going out through the roof. 22nd Act on impulse, you could be surprised how much it helps you to do so. 29-30th The end of the month could bring a sigh of relief in some ways. OPPORTUNITIES: 18-20th Perk up these days by making the most of social possibilities that are on offer. LIMITING INFLUENCES: 5-6th Life is slower and benefits are not too easy to come by.

PISCES BORN PEOPLE

OCTOBER   INFLUENCES: 1-2nd Although the month starts well you may feel that you want to slow things down a little. 12-13th Confidence is not high and you would respond well to some good, sound advice at this time. 22nd Act according to your conscience in a personal sense. 29th Details prove awkward, though probably not for long. OPPORTUNITIES: 16-17th It's easy to wear a smile now, and to instinctively do the right thing. LIMITING INFLUENCES: 3-4th Hard to be rational, so take a break from responsibility if you can.

NOVEMBER   INFLUENCES: 2-3rd Practicalities blot out too much enjoyment as the month commences. 10-11th With a mixture of practical commonsense and intuition, you can achieve much now. 22-23rd Not everyone wants to lend you a helping hand, though most folk will. 28-29th Go with the flow concerning issues that you are not really too concerned about. OPPORTUNITIES: 12-13th Everyone pitches in during this most entertaining and useful period. LIMITING INFLUENCES: 19-20th Doing what you really want is almost impossible just for the moment and patience eludes you.

DECEMBER   INFLUENCES: 2-3rd Most Pisceans are very domestically inclined for now and may stay close to home. 12-13th Confidence is on the increase again, so help yourself in some way. 27-28th Once Christmas is out of the way you can afford to slow things down a little. OPPORTUNITIES: 9-10th Utilise the good ideas that you have now to help not only your own causes but those of others too. LIMITING INFLUENCES: 24-25th Perhaps a quieter Christmas than you might have thought and family matters demand your attention.

ARIES BORN PEOPLE

Birthdays between March 21st and April 20th inclusive. Your planet is Mars. Birthstone, diamond. Lucky day, Tuesday.

KEYNOTE FOR THE YEAR   *Perhaps a slightly more settled year than the last couple, though still showing avenues of escape from routines. Romance flourishes.*

JANUARY   INFLUENCES: 4-5th Attend to finances and look after family matters to ensure ultimate success. 14-15th Social possibilities look more exciting than has been the case for a while. Comfort and security are more likely now. OPPORTUNITIES: 12th Ideal time for shopping and for looking out a bargain of some sort. 26th Career prospects reach a peak. LIMITING INFLUENCES: 19th A restricting period for personal relationships, take things steadily and don't rush your fences.

FEBRUARY   INFLUENCES: 1-2nd The unexpected grabs your attention now. 18-19th Sympathy shown to others is repaid significantly. 28th A time for getting what you need, though not what you want. OPPORTUNITIES: 14-15th Good prospects in terms of luck and money, though not a time to take too many chances. 22nd Advertise your professional presence and look out for new professional offers. LIMITING INFLUENCES: 12th Principles may prove to be too important and you could try too hard to make your point.

MARCH   INFLUENCES: 5-6th Refusing to be rushed, progress is indicated but flexibility could be better. 15-17th Much energy and a renewed determination generally comes your way at present. 20th A continued upswing in your social life can be very useful. OPPORTUNITIES: 13-14th Minor confrontations lead to significant gains financially, perhaps as a result of things you learn from the past. LIMITING INFLUENCES: 28-29th Low on energy, with a pronounced and quite definite need to take some rest.

ARIES BORN PEOPLE

APRIL INFLUENCES: Changing finances bring alterations in attitude and the ability to take some small chances. 15-16th Helpful news is now in the offing socially and friends prove to be especially helpful. 20th Fulfilment through material gains and new love. OPPORTUNITIES: 10-11th Back your hunches to achieve good results both now and in the days that lie ahead. LIMITING INFLUENCES: 24-25th A slower than usual period, some fatigue is likely and can be countered by a willingness to take some rest.

MAY INFLUENCES: 2-3rd Teamwork is very well accented. Look for groups or associations that need your support. 14-15th A time to make changes around the home and to improve your life-style as a result. 25th Casual ideas carry great possibilities for personal advancement. OPPORTUNITIES: 7-9th Look for new working prospects or even a change of direction. LIMITING INFLUENCES: 21-22nd Little real progress in a practical sense, though you can count on some support from relatives or friends.

JUNE INFLUENCES: 6-7th A little give and take works wonders with wayward relatives. 17th A period to allow your personality to take over and to make an impression in company. 28th Don't doubt your real influence. OPPORTUNITIES: 8-9th Time to look at summer travel and to plan outings that can take place in the near future. LIMITING INFLUENCES: 18-19th Negative indications coming from loved ones. Take note but don't react. 30th Keep investments to a minimum at present.

JULY INFLUENCES: 7-8th Positive thinking can be a real advantage and brings unexpected dividends. 15-16th Make the most of a good ability to put your point of view across to those around you. 26-27th Social commitments look like being demanding but can bring real enjoyment. OPPORTUNITIES: 3-4th Take the odd chance financially and don't be side-tracked by negative types who surround you now. LIMITING INFLUENCES: 18-19th Too slow to take advantage of very real possibilities for advancement.

AUGUST INFLUENCES: 6-7th Sudden changes in direction can be turned to your advantage, especially at work. 13th Fresh plans for a change of direction receive significant support. 24-25th Make the most of people who have a vested interest in seeing you succeed. Count on natural luck. OPPORTUNITIES: 1-2nd The best period of the month for showing your personal feelings and for stimulating romantic attachments. LIMITING INFLUENCES: 15-16th Confusion comes from the direction of your parter.

SEPTEMBER INFLUENCES: 2-3rd A very lively atmosphere socially invites you to take a more prominent role. 18-19th Powers of communication are excellent, don't keep your opinions to yourself. 27th Past emotional issues replay in your mind and can be turned to your advantage. OPPORTUNITIES: 24-26th A very healthy phase and one that helps you to see things in the way that friends do. LIMITING INFLUENCES: 11-12th No matter how passionate you may be yourself at this time, it is unlikely that others would reciprocate.

OCTOBER INFLUENCES: 6-7th An important time for planning, especially since friends are willing to join in and help. 18th Don't miss this important chance to get others working on your behalf, inside and outside of work. 24-26th Financial gains are now in the offing but tread carefully. OPPORTUNITIES: 21-22nd Gratitude comes your way and shows itself in some tangible ways. Compliments are flooding in too. LIMITING INFLUENCES: 8-9th Too much work could get you down at present, get some rest.

NOVEMBER INFLUENCES: 7-8th A good time to be getting on with new individuals and people with influence. 18-19th Plan a journey or even undertake one for maximum benefit. 27-28th There is the ability to win great respect from others, which could lead to advancement. OPPORTUNITIES: 15-16th An upturn in the way that you are able to affect your own longer-term destiny. better control of finances. LIMITING INFLUENCES: 29-30th Too much waiting around could see jobs losing impetus.

DECEMBER INFLUENCES: 6-7th A wonderful time for all manner of co-operative ventures and for making more of yourself socially. 13th Even people who normally shun you now begin to see you in a more favourable light. 29th the best time of the month for organising practical issues and for making life go with a swing. OPPORTUNITIES: 11-12th Even situations of confrontation can be turned to your advantage now. LIMITING INFLUENCES 26-27th You can be too opinionated for your own good.

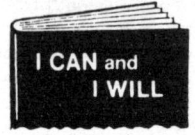

TAURUS BORN PEOPLE

Birthdays between April 21st and May 21st inclusive. Your planet is Venus. Birthstone, emerald. Lucky day, Friday.

KEYNOTE FOR THE YEAR   A greater degree of freedom is what you are really looking for as the year commences, and it is something that you work hard towards in the first part of the year. Romance looks likely in the late summer.

JANUARY   INFLUENCES: 7-8th Deal with practicalities and leave abstract situations until later. 13-14th High spirits are now in evidence and romance begins to take off. 27-28th A period for rest and relaxation. Continue to monitor financial out-goings. OPPORTUNITIES: 16-17th People with real influence now begin to cross your path and can bring new possibilities. LIMITING INFLUENCES: 2-3rd A little below par generally, not the best time to be taking on more than you really have to.

FEBRUARY   INFLUENCES: 2-3rd Although it's back to basics financially, there should be more about than you think. 14-15th Some initial conflict means a better understanding in the fullness of time. 28th Finish the month with a flourish, you can really make an impression now on almost anyone you meet. OPPORTUNITIES: 17-18th The Moon is in just the right position now to improve your general luck and to make you more confident. LIMITING INFLUENCES: 3-4th Less than average influence over important types.

MARCH   INFLUENCES: 5th A good day to allow yourself the right to your own opinion, don't be held back personally. 14-15th Contrary opinions make it difficult to make up your mind but life remains basically settled. 29th Now less restless, you can settle to some hard work. OPPORTUNITIES: 16-17th In the company of like-minded people it is possible to find new financial outlets. LIMITING INFLUENCES: 2-3rd What you are told and the genuine truth can be two different things at this time.

APRIL   INFLUENCES: 5-6th A very practical Taurean can make significant progress in practical situations. 15-16th Both these days should be especially good in terms of relationships and general financial progress. 29th A very busy interlude, though with enough time to stop and think if you wish to do so. OPPORTUNITIES: 12-14th Time to calculate odds before you embark on any kind of speculation. Once committed, you should do well. LIMITING INFLUENCES: 26-27th Personal friends prove very awkward.

MAY   INFLUENCES: 3-4th It is when you are close to home that the best opportunities present themselves. 18-19th A busy interlude, though one that holds some significant opportunities for personal growth. Friendships take a turn for the better and love rings some bells too. OPPORTUNITIES: 10-11th Treat yourself to a night out or a project you have been putting off for a while. LIMITING INFLUENCES: 23-24th It seems as though good luck is absent now.

JUNE   INFLUENCES: 4-5th Optimism is everything to Taurus at present, so don't look on the glum side of life. 17th A boost to personal finances should soon be showing itself to be a possibility. 27th A particularly active and interesting phase now begins professionally. OPPORTUNITIES: 6-7th If you are looking for comfort and security, now is the time to find your heart's desire. LIMITING INFLUENCES: 20-21st It appears that not everyone has confidence in you.

JULY   INFLUENCES: 6-7th Avoid overwork but at the same time keep an open mind about the possibility of advancement. 15-16th Progress is made at work and there should also be time for new social encounters. 25-26th Get-togethers and chance encounters lift the quality of life and bring financial rewards along with them. OPPORTUNITIES: 4-5th A strong conscience and a need to help show what an idealistic person you are. LIMITING INFLUENCES: 17-18th Too much inclination to back-down under pressure.

TAURUS BORN PEOPLE

AUGUST INFLUENCES: 2-3rd Taureans are good company now and can be great support to friends. 10-11th A good time for travel and for planning journeys later in the year. 17th Routines are a drag and you should look at life in a new way. 29-30th Home-loving and warm in your attitudes to others. OPPORTUNITIES: 1st, 27-28th Better financial potential and the chance for greater responsibility. LIMITING INFLUENCES: 13-14th Confidence to do what you know to be the right thing could be lacking now.

SEPTEMBER INFLUENCES: 1-2nd It becomes gradually less difficult to express yourself at present and friends are very supportive. 15-16th An 'anything could happen' sort of time, exciting and stimulating. 26-27th Stay in tune with others and don't be afraid to communicate while Mercury is around to offer help and support. OPPORTUNITIES: 23-24th Greater bounce-back sees you turning even difficult circumstances round to your own point of view. LIMITING INFLUENCES: 10-11th Think carefully before speaking out.

OCTOBER INFLUENCES: 3-4th Life proves to be a balancing act, though one you cope with easily at present. 10-11th Spreading yourself thinly at present you could be accused of not concentrating on any one aspect enough. 28-29th A variety of interests is still around but now choosing is less difficult. OPPORTUNITIES: 20-21st Great steps forward are likely, plus the chance of making a new start romantically. LIMITING INFLUENCES: 8-9th You need to rely on others but they are not around when you need them.

NOVEMBER INFLUENCES: 7-8th A new enterprise offers an enlightening interlude and friends prove to be very supportive. 22-23rd The changing position of the Sun makes you more supportive and improves reliability. 27-28th Unexpected financial demands gather, though with common-sense you can sort them out. OPPORTUNITIES: 17-18th Guesses are out of the window and you need to assert yourself positively. LIMITING INFLUENCES: 3-4th Partnerships bring problems to attached Taureans.

DECEMBER INFLUENCES: 2-3rd Outstanding jobs should be undertaken now. 5-6th Social mixing is important, with new people coming into your life. 17th Finances are apt to be on your mind but do think things through carefully. 26th Slow things down after Christmas and enjoy a well-earned break. OPPORTUNITIES: 14-15th Pre-planning for Christmas pays dividends. LIMITING INFLUENCES 28-29th Post-Christmas blues should be ignored, in favour of positive action.

GEMINI BORN PEOPLE

Birthdays between May 22nd and June 21st inclusive. Your planet is Mercury. Birthstone, agate. Lucky day, Wednesday.

KEYNOTE FOR THE YEAR   A year of significant practical progress lies ahead, though not if you allow yourself to be distracted by minor issues personally or spend too much time worrying about money.

JANUARY INFLUENCES: 1-2nd A quieter start to the year than you may have expected, but potentially productive. 10-11th Confidence is on the increase to do the right thing in all circumstances. 21st A short interlude of significant luck, take advantage of the fact. OPPORTUNITIES: 14-15th New incentives stand all around you and for once you are able to recognise them. LIMITING INFLUENCES: 5-6th A tendency to withdraw into yourself too much and to lose out as a result.

GEMINI BORN PEOPLE

FEBRUARY INFLUENCES: 5th Home-base matters take up much of your time, but happiness is possible. 12-13th Less incentive to succeed comes as a result of too much prior planning; and little spontaneous action. 28th Finish the month with a flourish, now you can look well ahead and make the most of the help that is on offer. OPPORTUNITIES: 19-20th A sunny and happy Gemini should make short work of any tasks that are piling up. LIMITING INFLUENCES: 3-4th Even small obstacles seem difficult to get round at this time.

MARCH INFLUENCES: 4-5th A somewhat caustic attitude does not help you to get ahead in a general sense. 9th Routines become less of a chore and you begin to show significantly more optimism. 22-23rd Definitely a time for keeping secrets, not everyone can be trusted during these days. OPPORTUNITIES: 19-20th Life is very eventful and you throw yourself into the thick of all sorts of activities. LIMITING INFLUENCES: 1-2nd The reliability of information that comes your way is doubtful.

APRIL INFLUENCES: 1-2nd Social trends start to look good as the month opens and you are in a position to gain from friendships. 9-10th Routines mean having to put yourself out and are not especially comfortable. 23-24th Confirming past suspicions puts you firmly in the driving seat where personal aspects are concerned. OPPORTUNITIES: 16-17th Masses of confidence comes your way, a time to really get moving. LIMITING INFLUENCES: 28-29th Not a time to push the boat out or for taking risks.

MAY INFLUENCES: 4-5th An unusual time, though more enterprising and exciting than for some time. 9-10th Despite promising starts in one or two directions, delays are inevitable. 29-30th New starts beckon on the work front and relationships take a turn for the better. OPPORTUNITIES: 12-14th Optimism, vigour and enterprise are all waiting for you to recognise their presence. 25-26th LIMITING INFLUENCES: Unexpected happenings cause delays that you can do little about.

JUNE INFLUENCES: 3-4th The best time of the month for making up your mind about finances and how to deal with them. 12-13th Easy to get along with friends and to bring them round to your ideas. 26-27th A good time for basics and for prior planning in a career sense. OPPORTUNITIES: 8-9th High spirits find you in the mood for change and diversity. LIMITING INFLUENCES: 22-23rd A general slowing down of trends means that you have to accept second best for a while.

JULY INFLUENCES: 1-2nd Your powers of communication now seem to be at an all-time high and friends are supportive. 11-12th Promising incentives at work need some careful planning. 22-23rd Care is required in practical matters, though these are generally favourable. OPPORTUNITIES: 6-7th A get up and go attitude makes life easy in personal and professional directions. LIMITING INFLUENCES: 19-20th False starts are possible now and some extra care is necessary.

AUGUST INFLUENCES: 1st A quiet start to what turns out to be a particularly rewarding month ahead. 14th A good day for going it alone in personal plans and ambitions. 22-23rd With a very inventive phase now upon you, a good time for new incentives. OPPORTUNITIES: 2-3rd No need to think too deeply about things, just do what your intuition tells you to. LIMITING INFLUENCES: 15-17th Compromise is quite difficult and you could be too demanding of others.

SEPTEMBER INFLUENCES: 1-2nd Not a bad start to the month, though there are some awkward people about and you have to deal with them. 9-10th A more confident Gemini greets the day. Attitudes are variable. 21st Be prepared for a sudden hectic spell. 29th Controversy can be turned to your advantage. OPPORTUNITIES: 26-27th Support is on hand from many different directions, don't be afraid to use it. LIMITING INFLUENCES: 13-14th Delays in social adventures and new romantic proposals look inevitable.

OCTOBER INFLUENCES: 4-5th Speak your mind and expect those around you to understand your motivation. 17-18th Gemini is very intense at present, though this turns out to be a good thing. 30-31st People are conveniently placed to be of significant assistance just at the moment. OPPORTUNITIES: 24-25th Problems from the past can be solved in half the usual time, thanks to patience on your part. LIMITING INFLUENCES: 9-10th Not too brave at present, you tend to shy away from problems.

NOVEMBER INFLUENCES: 1-2nd Ambitions are obvious, the only thing you might lack is the ability to put them into practice. 9th A sunny day, at least inside you. A good period for a change or a journey. 22-23rd Keep talking, that way you should end up getting what you want from life. OPPORTUNITIES: 19-20th Almost anything that you decide to do can be turned to your advantage and enlists support. LIMITING INFLUENCES: 26-27th Some confusion at home overflows into various other areas of your life.

DECEMBER INFLUENCES: 3-4th A quicker pace of life and some happy coincidences should favour you greatly, avoid being hesitant. 14-15th Look for some important and far-reaching compromises. 24th Less incentive now, but more in the way of personal choice. OPPORTUNITIES: 16-18th Views that you have held for quite some time now make more sense. LIMITING INFLUENCES: 30-31st Not too easy to get your own way at present, in fact it isn't too sensible to try.

 # CANCER BORN PEOPLE

Birthdays between June 22nd and July 22nd inclusive. Your planet is the Moon. Birthstone, ruby. Lucky day, Monday.

KEYNOTE FOR THE YEAR   Progress is slower at the start of the year, though it is to the area of personal matters and improved finances that you find your mind turning in the fullness of time. New work possibilities follow.

JANUARY INFLUENCES: 1-2nd Divided loyalties could be something of a problem at the start of the year but keep an open mind. 11-12th Look out for small details that have far-reaching implications. Important matters look after themselves. 27-28th Communication is very important and leads to significant gains. OPPORTUNITIES: 24-25th You know yourself extremely well at this time and make sensible decisions. LIMITING INFLUENCES: 9-10th Routines are inclined to hold you back.

FEBRUARY INFLUENCES: 2-3rd Not a progressive phase, but a useful one for pleasing yourself and for helping friends out. 17th A very good period for taking a journey and one in which the unusual grabs your attention. 25-26th Don't give in to temporary pessimism and be bold in your actions. OPPORTUNITIES: 21-22nd Satisfying encounters come along and improve your social life no end. LIMITING INFLUENCES: 7-8th The Crab is crawling back into its shell in no uncertain terms now.

MARCH INFLUENCES: 4-5th Although you hold tightly to what you know, life does carry advantages. 10-11th More outgoing now and able to see the point of view put across by those in your immediate vicinity. 29-30th End of the month initiatives captivate your imagination more than ever. OPPORTUNITIES: 21-22nd Virtue turns out to be its own reward at this time. LIMITING INFLUENCES: 7-8th There is no point in having to rehearse what you want to say, though you do so anyway.

APRIL INFLUENCES: 1-2nd Personal disputes cloud this period a little, though only if you are willing to allow them to do so. 15-16th Mid-month opportunities look like improving your financial lot more than ever. 29-30th A good time for travel and for pleasing yourself over personal details. OPPORTUNITIES: 17-19th A highly productive period, with plenty to keep you both occupied and happy. LIMITING INFLUENCES: 3-4th Real happiness at this time is quite elusive and optimism is hard to find.

MAY 3-4th Easy now to come to terms with changes though not everyone follows your particular reasoning. 19-20th The Crab takes a back seat in many situations right now but does find the time to take a well-earned rest. 29-30th Prepare for a change of scene or even possibly a change of address. OPPORTUNITIES: 15-16th New people come into your life and alter your thinking for the better. LIMITING INFLUENCES: 27-28th Vital information is misunderstood unless you concentrate on what is being said.

CANCER BORN PEOPLE

JUNE INFLUENCES: 1-2nd Not a dynamic start to the year, though there are personal advantages on the way. 14-15th A smooth passage through changes undertaken at work. 27-28th Less pressure from relatives now, though more from friends. OPPORTUNITIES: 11-12th A dynamic approach to spending and investment would be useful at this time. LIMITING INFLUENCES: 24-25th It isn't your own behaviour that is likely to be causing you any problems at present, more the general attitudes of others.

JULY INFLUENCES: 1-2nd Little time to relax or to do what takes your fancy, though plenty of gains to be made on the way. 10-11th gains are possible in a career sense, but do be careful not to over-state your case now. 30-31st Congratulations may be in order somewhere within the family. OPPORTU-NITIES: 8-9th Although you are now only too willing to speak your mind, others will agree with you generally. LIMITING INFLUENCES: 21-22nd Any personal satisfaction is hard to find.

AUGUST INFLUENCES: 1-2nd Don't hold too hard to what is yours and make great gains as a result. 11-12th Constant attention to detail could be rather tiring, so take an over-view when possible. 28-29th Nearing the end of the month you could be feeling just a little insecure. OPPORTUNITIES: 5-6th Grant yourself the right to be correct in your judgements, chances are that you really are. LIMITING INFLUENCES: 18-19th Personal reproaches coming from the direction of friends could be hard to deal with.

SEPTEMBER INFLUENCES: 4-5th Possibly the most socially rewarding part of the month. Good for new ventures and all forms of travel. 17-18th Not everyone is on your wavelength, but the most important people are. 30th Things could be quieter, but at least you have the time to think. OPPORTU-NITIES: 28-29th Use your creative skills to rebuild parts of your world that are not to your liking. LIM-ITING INFLUENCES: 14-15th Not everyone is being quite as helpful as they could be for the moment, so patience is called for.

OCTOBER INFLUENCES: 1-2nd Personal disputes are likely at the beginning of the month, don't allow these to divert your attention. 14-15th Don't allow others to gain control over your own resources right now. 28-29th A wait and see attitude would be best when it comes to changes promised regarding your working life. OPPORTUNITIES: 25-27th Confidence to do what takes your fancy is now very high and others will certainly join in. LIMITING INFLUENCES: 11-12th Not a good time for gambling or taking the initiative.

NOVEMBER INFLUENCES: 2-3rd An unusual phase, and one where your own hunches can be fol-lowed almost totally. 11-12th You may be holding too tightly to the family purse-strings now and need to be a little more flexible. 29-30th At work you should stick to what you know and try to remain practi-cal in a general sense. OPPORTUNITIES: 22-23rd Plenty to talk about and no shortage of communica-tion skills to do it. LIMITING INFLUENCES: 7-8th In any form of speculation the odds are stacked against you now.

DECEMBER INFLUENCES: 1-2nd Set your sights high personally and professionally at the start of a progressive month. 7-8th Single Cancerians especially should warm to the new romantic prospects that are in the offing. 30-31st You are on top form to look ahead to a bright period at the start of the new year. OPPORTUNITIES: 19-20th Plenty of time to do what you want, and good organisational skills LIMITING INFLUENCES: 5-6th Money could be short, so make certain you spend wisely.

 # LEO BORN PEOPLE

Birthdays between July 23rd and August 23rd inclusive. Your planet is the Sun. Birthstone, sapphire. Lucky day, Sunday.

KEYNOTE FOR THE YEAR   Emotionally speaking, the more demonstrative you allow yourself to be at the start of the year, the better things should be in the long-run. A good period for moving towards prac-tical objectives in a considered manner.

. .32. .

LEO BORN PEOPLE

JANUARY   INFLUENCES: 1-2nd Make the most of the start of the year by laying down plans especially carefully. 14-15th The Lion is very showy at the moment, but do look for some modesty. 30-31st Some anxiety regarding family members or a friend is understandable, though not especially necessary. OPPORTUNITIES: 28-29th Your life responds well to new input and the positive attitude you are adopting. LIMITING INFLUENCES: 11-12th Constraints are put upon spending, especially regarding luxuries.

FEBRUARY   INFLUENCES: 3-4th The arrival of a happy-go-lucky attitude proves to be especially useful at this time. 13-14th Since nobody knows you as well as you know yourself, do what comes naturally. 28th Perhaps not an especially exciting time, though one that proves excellent for prior-planning. OPPORTUNITIES: 24-25th Look out for new incentives at work and regarding finances. LIMITING INFLUENCES: 9-10th A continued reliance on others leads to some disappointments unless you are careful.

MARCH   INFLUENCES: 1-2nd Don't hide your light under a bushel as the month opens, be bold in everything you do. 11-12th A particularly good time for leisure pursuits and for showing yourself off to the world. 26-27th You are feeling rather unconventional and will be inclined to break out of routines. OPPORTUNITIES: 23-25th Enthusiasm acts as the spring-board to a number of new ventures that are on offer. LIMITING INFLUENCES: 9-10th Delays seem inevitable, fighting against them won't help.

APRIL   INFLUENCES: 1-2nd Start the month with a bright and breezy attitude as life goes your way generally. 17-18th Friends are only too willing to point out your faults. 24- 25th Routines can be a drag unless you ring the changes. 29-30th Congratulations could be in order somewhere in the family. OPPORTUNITIES: 20-21st Past efforts fund present and future gains personally. LIMITING INFLUENCES: 5-6th Life seems to be full of contradictions.

MAY   INFLUENCES: 1-2nd Things are starting to quieten down a little, enjoy the rest! 15-16th Create a comfortable world for the people you care about the most. 24-25th Confidence-boosting exercises turn out to your distinct advantage. OPPORTUNITIES: 17-18th Even people who have not supported you willingly in the past tend to do so at this time. LIMITING INFLUENCES: 3-4th You will need to be very careful in the way that you handle family members and good friends.

JUNE   INFLUENCES: 4-5th After a quiet start to the month, things now begin to speed up somewhat. 9-10th Plenty of scope for change and especially for travel. 29-30th There are some real personalities about and they cheer up your life no end. OPPORTUNITIES: 13-14th With careful thought you can turn most situations round to your way of thinking and should find finances to be stronger. LIMITING INFLUENCES: 26-27th There could be complaints about your unusual attitude towards others.

JULY   INFLUENCES: 1-2nd A good time to allow your natural personality to really shine out. 10-11th Relationships are important now, so look after them carefully. 21-22nd travel may be uppermost in your mind, so plan a journey. OPPORTUNITIES: 13-14th Most of what you have on your mind now makes real sense to others too. People seek out your timely advice. LIMITING INFLUENCES: 26-27th Restrictions crop up in your personal life and you will need to co-operate to avoid problems.

AUGUST   INFLUENCES: 1-2nd Getting along with others could not be easier but don't take them for granted. 16-17th High expectations may not be entirely fulfilled but you can have your own way generally. 27-29th People from the past crop up in your life again and need some special attention. OPPORTUNITIES: 10-12th the best time of the month to get your own way and to put new ideas into practice. LIMITING INFLUENCES: 23-25th Arguments seem to be fairly inevitable for a day or two.

SEPTEMBER   INFLUENCES: 4-5th Career prospects look especially good for the moment and you might be chasing a rise in salary. 18-19th Blessings come out of the blue, take advantage of them! 25-26th Get round potential problems by dealing with them early. OPPORTUNITIES: 2-3rd Confidence to do the right thing is especially high at present. LIMITING INFLUENCES; 16-17th Unusual complications could hold you back for a while, though not if you are circumspect.

                                              Cont'd on p. 48

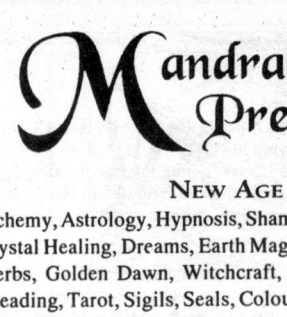

. .34. .

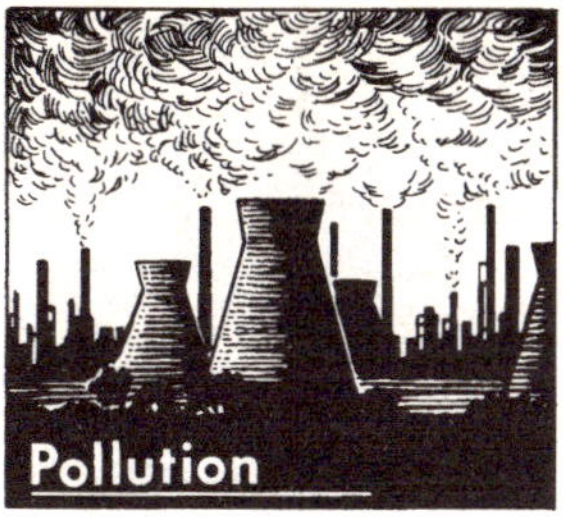

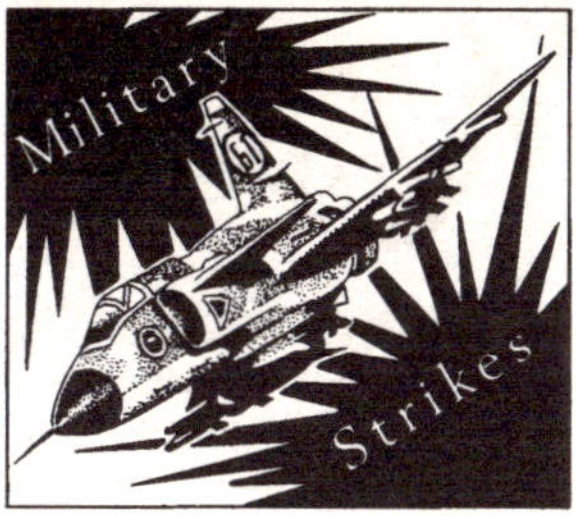

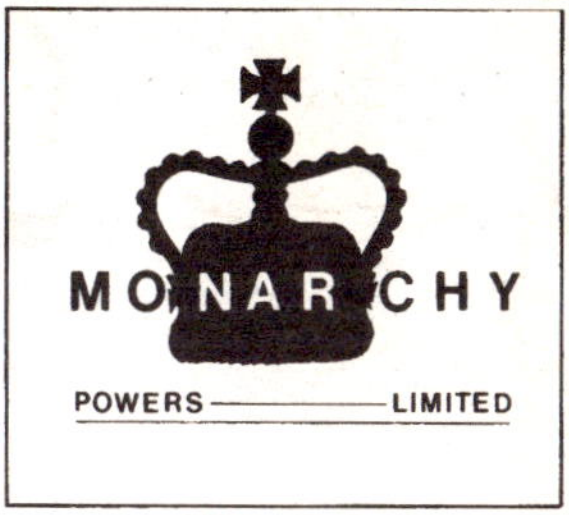

JANUARY

For High Water add, for Bristol 5h. 30m., Hull 4h. 23m., Leith 0h. 43m., and for Dublin sub. 2h. 21m., Greenock 1h. 22m., Liverpool 2h. 29m.

D of M	D of W	Sundays, Festivals Special Events, etc, for 1994	Sun Rises R Sets S	High Water at London Bridge		Moon at London		Weather
				Morn.	After.	Rises	Sets	
			h. m.	h. m.	h. m.	h. m.	h. m.	
1	S	New Year's Day	S16 02	3 45	16 10	20 45	9 38	A very mixed month with gales and spells of heavy rain during the first half. From mid-month it will be much colder with snow in many areas.
2	S	2nd Sun. after Christmas	R 8 06	4 23	16 51	22 03	10 02	
3	M	Bank Holiday	S16 04	5 02	17 33	23 21	10 25	
4	Tu	Salt II agreement 1993	R 8 05	5 43	18 21	—	10 48	
5	W	Amy Johnson's crash 1941	S16 06	6 32	19 17	0 40	11 14	
6	Th	Epiphany/Twelfth Night	R 8 05	7 33	20 26	1 59	11 43	
7	F	Cath. of Aragon d. 1536	S16 09	8 49	21 41	3 16	12 19	
8	S	B. of New Orleans 1815	R 8 04	10 09	22 54	4 30	13 03	
9	S	1st Sunday after Epiphany	S16 11	11 25	—	5 37	13 57	
10	M	London Underg'd op. 1863	R 8 03	0 01	12 31	6 33	15 00	
11	Tu	Albania a republic 1946	S16 14	0 57	13 24	7 18	16 09	
12	W	Nevil Shute d. 1960	R 8 01	1 47	14 12	7 54	17 21	
13	Th	Dallas airport op. 1974	S16 17	2 29	14 54	8 23	18 33	
14	F	Cecil Beaton b. 1904	R 8 00	3 08	15 34	8 47	19 43	
15	S	Top hat first worn 1779	S16 20	3 46	16 12	9 09	20 52	
16	S	2nd Sunday after Epiphany	R 7 58	4 21	16 48	9 28	21 59	
17	M	Thomas Crapper d. 1910	S16 23	4 55	17 23	9 47	23 04	
18	Tu	Sydney Greenstreet d. 1954	R 7 56	5 29	18 01	10 07	—	
19	W	Simon Rattle b. 1955	S16 26	6 07	18 42	10 29	0 09	
20	Th	Terry Waite abduct. 1987	R 7 54	6 53	19 31	10 54	1 14	
21	F	Lenin d. 1924	S16 30	7 48	20 30	11 23	2 18	
22	S	Anzio landings b'n 1944	R 7 52	8 54	21 32	11 59	3 20	
23	S	3rd Sunday after Epiphany	S16 33	10 00	22 37	12 44	4 19	
24	M	St Francis de Sales	R 7 50	11 08	23 42	13 38	5 12	
25	Tu	Burns Night	S16 37	—	12 11	14 41	5 59	
26	W	Republic Day, India	R 7 47	0 38	13 03	15 52	6 39	
27	Th	Lewis Carroll b. 1932	S16 40	1 26	13 48	17 08	7 12	
28	F	*Challenger* disaster 1986	R 7 45	2 09	14 32	18 26	7 41	
29	S	Alan Ladd d. 1964	S16 44	2 50	15 14	19 46	8 06	
30	S	Septuagesima Sunday	R 7 42	3 29	15 53	21 07	8 30	
31	M	Sam Goldwyn d. 1974	S16 47	4 07	16 34	22 27	8 54	

MOON'S PHASES JANUARY 1994

		Days	*Hrs.*	*Mins.*
☾	Last Quarter	5	0	1
●	New Moon	11	23	10
☽	First Quarter	19	20	27
○	Full Moon	27	13	23

All times on this page are GMT

PREDICTIONS

The New Moon on the 11th falls in an exact conjunction with Uranus, Neptune, Venus and Mars, representing a highly unstable start to the year. Governments will be influenced by ideals and fantasies rather than the good and prosperity of their people, and there is a high chance of revolutionary outbursts and military strikes. Government will be conducted by leak and there will be revelations of corruption and underhand activity. There is also an extremely high possibility of pollution accidents, including radiation, oil and gas leaks. In the UK the arguments are likely to centre on homelessness, uncertainty in the housing market and the continuing need for reform in local taxation. There will also be continuing pressure for constituional reform, including limiting the powers of the monarchy. The FTSE 1090 share index is likely to begin a fall of up to 20%, prior to returning economic confidence in the Spring. *The Full Moon on the 27th falls in Leo,* indicating arguments in the teaching profession and reform of the postal and telecommunications services. The Conservative party will be in disarray. The US navy will be in action overseas and there is the possibility of the Balkan war spreading.

Second favourites may be worth following at National Hunt race meetings.

The tidal predictions for London Bridge have been computed by the Proudman Oceanographic Laboratory.

Predicted Disintegration of Yugoslavia 1992

British Relations

Russian Army

IN ACTION

FEBRUARY

For High Water add, for Bristol 5h. 30m., Hull 4h. 23m., Leith 0h. 43m., and for Dublin sub. 2h. 21m., Greenock 1h. 22m., Liverpool 2h. 29m.

D of M	D of W	Sundays, Festivals Special Events, etc, for 1994	Sun Rises R Sets S	High Water at London Bridge		Moon at London		Weather
				Morn.	After.	Rises	Sets	
			h. m.	h. m.	h. m.	h. m.	h. m.	
1	Tu	Piet Mondrian d. 1944	R 7 39	4 45	17 16	23 47	9 20	
2	W	Cub Scouts founded 1914	S16 51	5 27	18 01	—	9 48	
3	Th	Woodrow Wilson d. 1924	R 7 36	6 12	18 52	1 05	10 22	
4	F	Guatemala 'quake 1976	S16 55	7 10	19 55	2 20	11 02	
5	S	Patty Hearst kidnap 1974	R 7 32	8 23	21 08	3 27	11 52	
6	�	Sexagesima Sunday	S16 58	9 45	22 27	4 26	12 50	
7	M	Grenada independent 1974	R 7 29	11 09	23 43	5 14	13 55	
8	Tu	Boy Scouts founded 1910	S17 02	—	12 18	5 53	15 05	
9	W	Adolphe Saxe b. 1894	R 7 26	0 43	13 13	6 24	16 16	
10	Th	Old Chinese New Year	S17 06	1 33	13 59	6 50	17 26	
11	F	Mary Quant b. 1934	R 7 22	2 13	14 39	7 13	18 35	
12	S	First day of Ramadan	S17 09	2 50	15 15	7 33	19 43	
13	☽	Quinquagesima Sunday	R 7 18	3 24	15 48	7 53	20 49	
14	M	St Valentine's Day	S17 13	3 55	16 19	8 13	21 54	
15	Tu	Shrove Tuesday	R 7 14	4 26	16 49	8 34	22 59	
16	W	Ash Wednesday	S17 17	4 57	17 22	8 57	—	
17	Th	Alan Bates b. 1934	R 7 11	5 32	17 58	9 24	0 03	
18	F	Andrés Segovia b. 1894	S17 20	6 11	18 38	9 57	1 05	
19	S	Duke of York b. 1960	R 7 07	6 56	19 26	10 37	2 04	
20	☽	1st Sunday in Lent	S17 24	7 52	20 27	11 25	2 59	
21	M	Robert Mugabe b. 1924	R 7 03	9 05	21 43	12 23	3 48	
22	Tu	Andy Warhol d. 1987	S17 27	10 26	23 04	13 29	4 31	
23	W	L. Baekeland d. 1944	R 6 59	11 42	—	14 42	5 07	
24	Th	Bobby Moore d. 1993	S17 31	0 10	12 39	15 59	5 38	
25	F	Clay k.o.'d Liston 1964	R 6 54	1 02	13 27	17 20	6 06	
26	S	Fats Domino b. 1928	S17 35	1 45	14 11	18 42	6 32	
27	☽	2nd Sunday in Lent	R 6 50	2 27	14 53	20 05	6 56	
28	M	Joan Greenwood d. 1987	S17 38	3 07	15 34	21 28	7 22	

A dry month with a good deal of sunshine but quite severe frosts. It will become very much milder towards the end of the month.

MOON'S PHASES FEBRUARY 1994		Days	Hrs.	Mins.
☾	Last Quarter	3	8	6
●	New Moon	10	14	30
☽	First Quarter	18	17	47
○	Full Moon	26	1	15

All times on this page are GMT

PREDICTIONS

The New Moon on the 10th will fall in Aquarius, indicating a need for banking and insurance reform in the UK. Venus square Pluto and Mercury conjunct Saturn indicate that international agreements should focus on long-term visions rather than details. In the UK the House of Lords is likely to challenge legislation from the Commons. There will be major reductions in public spending, mainly on the arts and welfare benefits. A major public announcement concerning British relations with the EEC could coincide with a currency realignment. China will be asserting its position as a leading economic power, and may be preparing to engage in a trade war. In Iran there could be an assassination attempt on a public figure, whilst for India there may be a change of government. Germany ushers in important constitutional change and the Russian army will be in action on the streets of a Russian city. *The Full Moon on the 26th will fall in Virgo* indicating continuing constitutional change in the UK, together with increased regulation of the private financial sector, whilst new reforms will be proposed to the teaching system. Iraq will be asserting itself as a regional leader in the Gulf.

The Tote Gold Trophy at Newbury may be won by a horse carrying 10st 10lbs.

See OLD MOORE'S Personal Horoscope, page 24

Predicted Russian Disintegration 1990

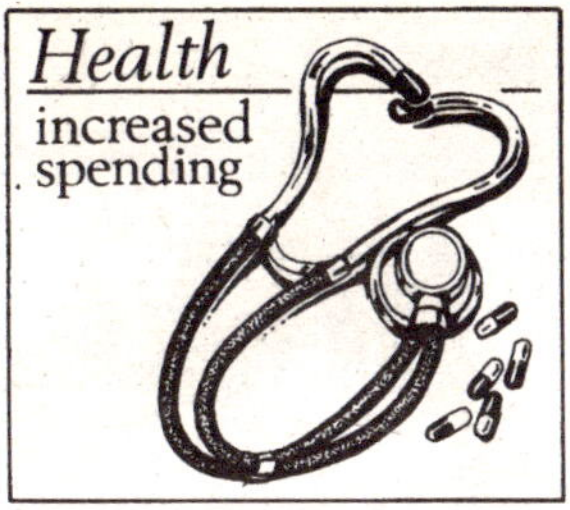

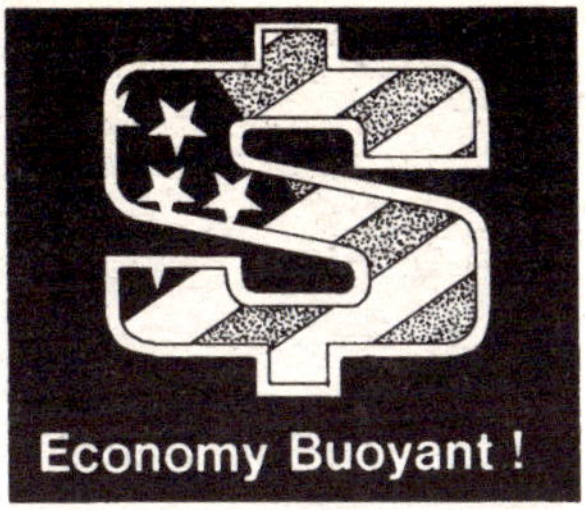

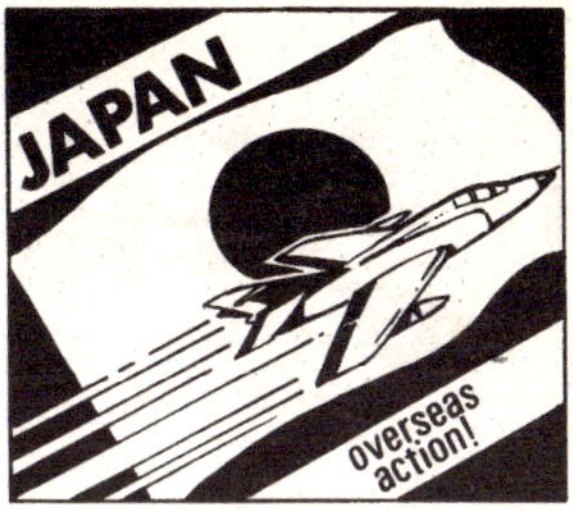

MARCH

For High Water add, for Bristol 5h. 30m., Hull 4h. 23m., Leith 0h. 43m., and for Dublin sub. 2h. 21m., Greenock 1h. 22m., Liverpool 2h. 29m.

D of M	D of W	Sundays, Festivals Special Events, etc, for 1994	Sun Rises R Sets S	High Water at London Bridge Morn.	High Water at London Bridge After.	Moon at London Rises	Moon at London Sets	Weather
			h. m.	h. m.	h. m.	h. m.	h. m.	
1	Tu	St David's Day	R 6 46	3 46	16 14	22 49	7 51	Generally cold during the first 10 days or so. Periods of rain around the middle of the month will be followed by squally gales.
2	W	Rhodesia a republic 1970	S17 42	4 27	16 57	—	8 24	
3	Th	Fatima Whitbread b. 1961	R 6 42	5 11	17 40	0 08	9 03	
4	F	Lincoln Handicap	S17 45	5 58	18 29	1 19	9 51	
5	S	Lord Ridley d. 1993	R 6 37	6 55	19 27	2 21	10 46	
6	𝔖	3rd Sunday in Lent	S17 49	8 04	20 37	3 12	11 49	
7	M	Royal Hort. Soc. f'd 1804	R 6 33	9 24	21 57	3 53	12 56	
8	Tu	Queen Anne access'n 1702	S17 52	10 49	23 20	4 26	14 5	
9	W	Yuri Gagarin b. 1934	R 6 28	—	12 00	4 54	15 15	
10	Th	Prince Edward b. 1964	S17 56	0 22	12 55	5 17	16 23	
11	F	Chelsea Hospital f'd 1682	R 6 24	1 12	13 40	5 38	17 30	
12	S	*Anschluss* 1938	S17 59	1 52	14 18	5 58	18 36	
13	𝔖	Mothering Sunday	R 6 19	2 27	14 50	6 18	19 42	
14	M	Commonwealth Day	S18 02	3 00	15 21	6 39	20 47	
15	Tu	Tommy Cooper d. 1984	R 6 15	3 28	15 48	7 02	21 51	
16	W	Leo McKern b. 1920	S18 06	3 56	16 16	7 28	22 53	
17	Th	St Patrick's Day	R 6 10	4 27	16 47	7 58	23 53	
18	F	Rimsky-Korsakov b. 1844	S18 09	5 02	17 20	8 35	—	
19	S	Pat. McGoohan b. 1928	R 6 06	5 39	17 57	9 19	0 49	
20	𝔖	Passion Sunday	S18 13	6 21	18 41	10 11	1 39	
21	M	St Benedict	R 6 01	7 12	19 34	11 11	2 23	
22	Tu	Stephen Sondheim b. 1930	S18 16	8 19	20 51	12 19	3 02	
23	W	Peter Lorre d. 1964	R 5 57	9 46	22 23	13 32	3 34	
24	Th	Orde Wingate d. 1944	S18 19	11 08	23 37	14 50	4 03	
25	F	Lady Day/The Annunciation	R 5 52	—	12 11	16 10	4 30	
26	S	Diana Ross b. 1944	S18 23	0 32	13 02	17 33	4 55	
27	𝔖	Palm Sunday/Pesach	R 5 47	1 19	13 47	18 57	5 21	
28	M	Stephen Leacock d. 1944	S18 26	2 02	14 29	20 22	5 49	
29	Tu	Oak Apple Day	R 5 43	2 43	15 11	21 45	6 21	
30	W	*Oklahoma!* première 1943	S18 29	3 25	15 53	23 02	6 59	
31	Th	Al Gore b. 1948	R 5 38	4 10	16 37	—	7 45	

MOON'S PHASES MARCH 1994

		Days	Hrs.	Mins.
☾	Last Quarter	4	16	53
●	New Moon	12	7	5
☽	First Quarter	20	12	14
○	Full Moon	27	11	10

All times GMT (BST from March 27 + 1 hour)

PREDICTIONS

The New Moon on the 12th falls in Pisces in the twelfth house at London, indicating expansion and increased expenditure on health and the prison services. There could also be new child abuse scandals. In general this is an auspicious moment for pursuing principles and dreams, but is not a favourable time for beginning new practical ventures. Relations between the UK and the EEC will deteriorate further. The US economy begins to look more buoyant. In the UK economic confidence should be returning, although the stock market is likely to dip after the 24th. Russia will be in an expansionist mood, increasing its influence overseas and protecting Russian minorities in other countries. Japanese troops may be called into action overseas. In the Middle East there could be a change of government in Egypt, whilst Iraq will be asserting itself and is likely to threaten one of its neighbours. There could be elections in South Africa and anti-government riots in Iran. *The Full Moon on the 27th falls in Libra* and is on the UK ascendant. This indicates a desire for popular change, and a confidence that democratic change is possible.

The Lincoln Handicap may be won by a horse carrying 8st 1lb and the Grand National by the favourite.

Clocks forward, 1 hour 27 March

OLD MOORE predicted the General Strike to the day — 3rd May 1926

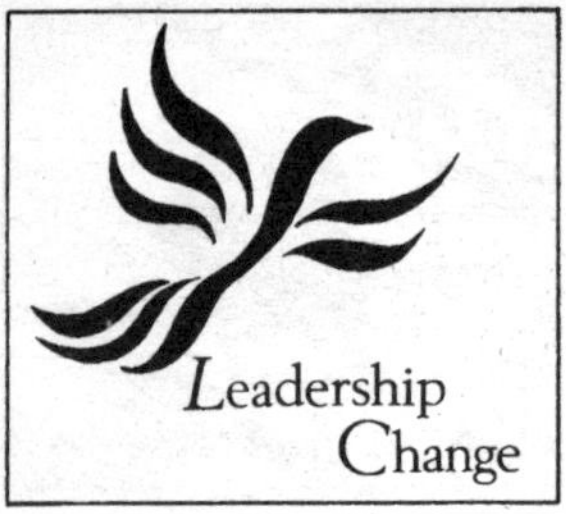

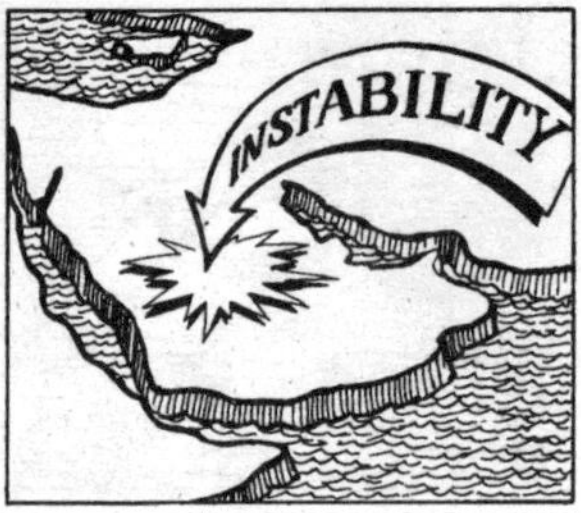

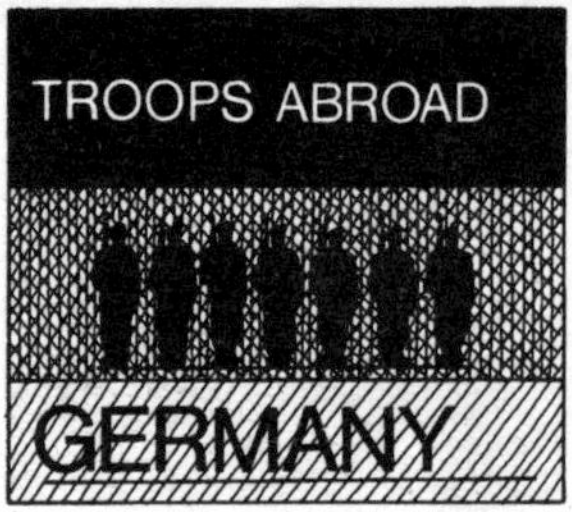

APRIL

For High Water add, for Bristol 5h. 30m., Hull 4h. 23m., Leith 0h. 43m., and for Dublin sub. 2h. 21m., Greenock 1h. 22m., Liverpool 2h. 29m.

D of M	D of W	Sundays, Festivals Special Events, etc, for 1994	Sun Rises R Sets S	High Water at London Bridge Morn.	High Water at London Bridge After.	Moon at London Rises	Moon at London Sets	Weather
			h. m.	h. m.	h. m.	h. m.	h. m.	
1	F	Good Friday	S18 33	4 57	17 22	0 10	8 40	A cold start with keen night frosts from the 1st-10th. It will then become warmer with some sunny Spring-like days and traditional April showers.
2	S	Sir Alec Guinness b. 1914	R 5 34	5 47	18 11	1 07	9 42	
3	S	Easter Day	S18 36	6 43	19 04	1 52	10 49	
4	M	Easter Monday	R 5 29	7 45	20 08	2 28	11 58	
5	Tu	Danton guillotined 1794	S18 40	8 58	21 24	2 57	13 07	
6	W	PAYE began 1944	R 5 25	10 23	22 51	3 22	14 15	
7	Th	Sir David Frost b. 1939	S18 43	11 34	23 56	3 44	15 22	
8	F	Emperor Caracalla d. 217	R 5 20	—	12 29	4 04	16 28	
9	S	Grand National	S18 46	0 46	13 13	4 24	17 33	
10	S	Low Sunday	R 5 16	1 27	13 51	4 44	18 37	
11	M	Napoleon abdicated 1814	S18 50	2 02	14 23	5 07	19 41	
12	Tu	*Tatler* first pub. 1709	R 5 12	2 32	14 51	5 31	20 44	
13	W	Amritsar massacre 1919	S18 53	3 00	15 17	6 01	21 45	
14	Th	Sir John Gielgud b. 1904	R 5 07	3 29	15 46	6 35	22 42	
15	F	Bessie Smith b. 1894	S18 56	4 02	16 17	7 16	23 34	
16	S	Anatole France b. 1844	R 5 03	4 37	16 52	8 05	—	
17	S	2nd Sunday after Easter	S19 00	5 15	17 29	9 02	0 20	
18	M	Paul Revere's ride 1775	R 4 59	5 57	18 10	10 05	0 59	
19	Tu	Pierre Curie d. 1906	S19 03	6 46	19 02	11 14	1 33	
20	W	Canaletto d. 1768	R 4 54	7 49	20 12	12 27	2 02	
21	Th	Elizabeth II b. 1926	S19 06	9 11	21 42	13 43	2 29	
22	F	R. Oppenheimer b. 1904	R 4 50	10 33	22 59	15 02	2 54	
23	S	St George's Day	S19 10	11 39	—	16 24	3 18	
24	S	3rd Sunday after Easter	R 4 46	0 00	12 34	17 48	3 45	
25	M	Anzac Day	S19 13	0 52	13 21	19 13	4 15	
26	Tu	Tanzania formed 1964	R 4 42	1 37	14 06	20 35	4 50	
27	W	Cecil Day-Lewis b. 1904	S19 16	2 22	14 50	21 50	5 33	
28	Th	1000 Guineas, Newmarket	R 4 38	3 08	15 35	22 54	6 25	
29	F	Zizi Jeanmaire b. 1924	S19 20	3 56	16 20	23 46	7 27	
30	S	2000 Guineas, Newmarket	R 4 34	4 45	17 06	—	8 35	

MOON'S PHASES APRIL 1994

		Days	*Hrs.*	*Mins.*
☾	Last Quarter	3	2	55
●	New Moon	11	0	17
☽	First Quarter	19	2	34
○	Full Moon	25	19	45

All times on this page are GMT (Add 1 hour BST)

PREDICTIONS

The New Moon on the 11th falls in Aries in a square to Uranus, Neptune and the UK Moon. The pressure for constitutional reform, focussing on the position of the monarchy, will be intensified once again. The concept of whether a Royal Family is necessary in addition to the monarchy is now under discussion. In addition, support for reform of the House of Lords and the electoral system will be growing stronger. The government will be lined up for heavy defeat in any local or parliamentary elections. There could also be changes in the leadership of the Liberal Democrats. The US will be involved in a naval war and there is the greatest risk of instability in Saudi Arabia, with a high probability of a change in leadership. Look towards a new government, with possible revolutionary fervour, in Iran. German peacekeeping troops could now be active abroad. *The Full Moon on the 25th falls in Scorpio and is strongly aspected to Mercury and Jupiter* indicating a major international conference, perhaps on health workers' rights and mobility of labour. The UK will be confident and following a belligerent foreign policy.

At Newbury the Greenham Stakes may be won by the second favourite, and at Newmarket the Craven Stakes may be won by the favourite.

Published EVERY YEAR since 1697

Predicted 2000 Guineas Winner 1993

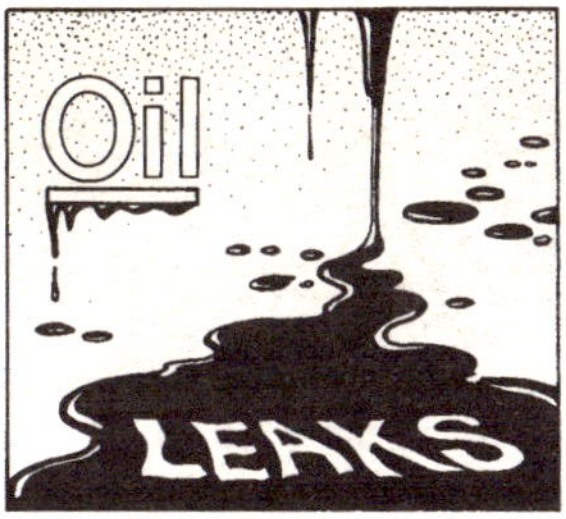

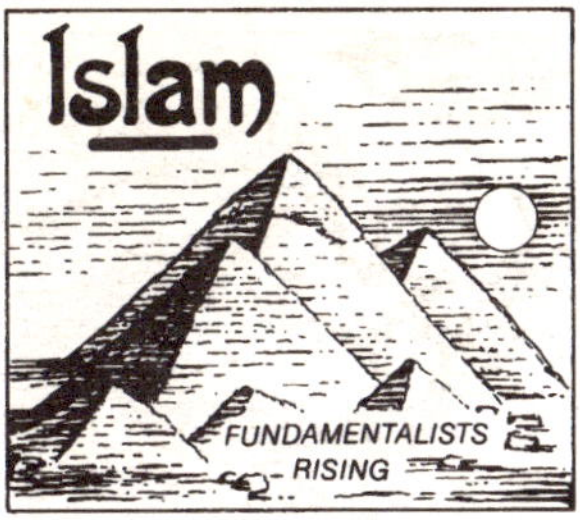

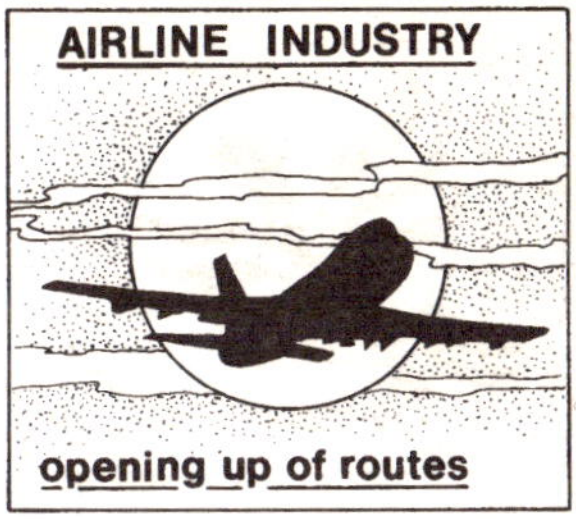

MAY

For High Water add, for Bristol 5h. 30m., Hull 4h. 23m., Leith 0h. 43m., and for Dublin sub. 2h. 21m., Greenock 1h. 22m., Liverpool 2h. 29m.

D of M	D of W	Sundays, Festivals Special Events, etc, for 1994	Sun Rises R Sets S	High Water at London Bridge Morn.	High Water at London Bridge After.	Moon at London Rises	Moon at London Sets	Weather
			h. m.	h. m.	h. m.	h. m.	h. m.	
1	S	4th Sunday after Easter	S19 23	5 36	17 54	0 27	9 46	After an unsettled start with heavy downpours the second half will blossom into warmer weather with a minor heatwave during the last week.
2	M	Bank Holiday	R 4 31	6 28	18 43	0 59	10 56	
3	Tu	R. D'Oyly Carte b. 1844	S19 26	7 24	19 40	1 26	12 06	
4	W	St Florian	R 4 27	8 27	20 46	1 49	13 13	
5	Th	Michael Palin b. 1943	S19 29	9 42	22 07	2 10	14 20	
6	F	Yale lock patent 1851	R 4 23	10 59	23 20	2 30	15 25	
7	S	Johannes Brahms b. 1833	S19 33	11 56	—	2 50	16 29	
8	S	Rogation Sunday	R 4 20	0 14	12 42	3 11	17 33	
9	M	Ulrike Meinhof d. 1976	S19 36	0 56	13 20	3 35	18 36	
10	Tu	Churchill became PM 1940	R 4 17	1 33	13 52	4 03	19 38	
11	W	Salvador Dali b. 1904	S19 39	2 04	14 22	4 36	20 37	
12	Th	Ascension Day	R 4 13	2 34	14 51	5 15	21 31	
13	F	Joe Louis b. 1914	S19 42	3 07	15 22	6 02	22 18	
14	S	Blackpool Tower op. 1894	R 4 10	3 42	15 57	6 56	22 59	
15	S	Ascension Sunday	S19 45	4 20	16 33	7 57	23 34	
16	M	Feast of Weeks (Shavuot)	R 4 07	4 59	17 09	9 03	—	
17	Tu	Mafeking relieved 1900	S19 48	5 40	17 50	10 13	0 05	
18	W	Monte Cassino taken 1944	R 4 04	6 28	18 39	11 26	0 31	
19	Th	Anne Boleyn exec. 1536	S19 51	7 27	19 42	12 41	0 56	
20	F	C. Columbus d. 1506	R 4 02	8 40	21 04	13 59	1 20	
21	S	FIFA founded 1904	S19 54	9 59	22 21	15 19	1 44	
22	S	Whit Sunday/Pentecost	R 3 59	11 08	23 29	16 42	2 11	
23	M	Bonnie and Clyde d. 1934	S19 56	—	12 07	18 04	2 43	
24	Tu	Brooklyn Bridge op. 1883	R 3 57	0 27	13 00	19 23	3 21	
25	W	Gustav Holst d. 1934	S19 59	1 19	13 48	20 34	4 08	
26	Th	George Formby b. 1904	R 3 54	2 08	14 33	21 34	5 06	
27	F	Pandit Nehru d. 1964	S20 02	2 56	15 19	22 21	6 13	
28	S	Eric Morcambe d. 1984	R 3 52	3 45	16 04	22 58	7 25	
29	S	Trinity Sunday	S20 04	4 33	16 49	23 28	8 38	
30	M	Bank Holiday	R 3 50	5 20	17 34	23 53	9 51	
31	Tu	Tintoretto d. 1594	S20 06	6 08	18 19	—	11 01	

MOON'S PHASES MAY 1994

		Days	Hrs.	Mins.
☾	Last Quarter	2	14	32
●	New Moon	10	17	7
☽	First Quarter	18	12	50
○	Full Moon	25	3	39

All times on this page are GMT (Add 1 hour BST)

PREDICTIONS

The New Moon, an eclipse on the 10th falls in Taurus on a degree which is very important for the future of Europe, and hopes for European union are liable to be thrown into turmoil, though temporarily. Mars square to Uranus and Neptune represents a risk of oil, gas and radiation leaks as well as leaks in government. A high degree of public anger suggest that the government's fortunes will slump. In the UK there will be reorganisation of agricultural subsidies and hopes of an end to the property slump. The government will introduce new trades union legislation and the Labour Party will be in a state of confusion. The Islamic fundamentalists will be rising in Egypt. Iraq is in danger of splitting into different regions, and there will be further anti-government demonstrations in Iran. There is a danger of changes of government in Jamaica and Japan, and leadership changes in South Africa. *The Full Moon on the 25th falls in Sagittarius,* indicating sudden developments in the air-line industry, an opening up of routes, lower fares and other ways of making public travel easier. China can expect leadership changes and instability will continue in Saudi Arabia.

At Newmarket the 2000 Guineas may be won by the second favourite and the 1000 Guineas by a French-trained filly.

10 May, annular Eclipse of the Sun, 14h. 12m — 20h. 11m

Predicted Oaks Winner 1993

Leadership Change

Israeli–Palestinian Settlement

JUNE

For High Water add, for Bristol 5h. 30m., Hull 4h. 23m., Leith 0h. 43m., and for Dublin sub. 2h. 21m., Greenock 1h. 22m., Liverpool 2h. 29m.

D of M	D of W	Sundays, Festivals Special Events, etc, for 1994	Sun Rises R Sets S	High Water at London Bridge Morn.	After.	Moon at London Rises	Sets	Weather
			h. m.	h. m.	h. m.	h. m.	h. m.	
1	W	The Derby, Epsom	R 3 49	6 57	19 07	0 15	12 08	
2	Th	Corpus Christi	S20 08	7 51	20 05	0 35	13 14	
3	F	Franz Kafka d. 1924	R 3 47	8 54	21 12	0 55	14 19	
4	S	Allies enter Rome 1944	S20 11	10 06	23 30	1 16	15 24	
5	�	1st Sunday after Trinity	R 3 46	11 13	23 34	1 39	16 27	
6	M	D-Day landings 1944	S20 12	—	12 04	2 06	17 30	
7	Tu	'Beau' Brummell b. 1778	R 3 45	0 22	12 46	2 37	18 30	
8	W	Millicent Martin b. 1934	S20 14	1 02	13 21	3 14	19 26	
9	Th	Lord Beaverbrook d. 1964	R 3 44	1 37	13 55	3 58	20 16	
10	F	Prince Philip b. 1921	S20 16	2 13	14 30	4 50	21 00	
11	S	The Queen's official b'day	R 3 43	2 50	15 07	5 50	21 37	
12	�	2nd Sunday after Trinity	S20 17	3 29	15 43	6 55	22 09	
13	M	First V-1 landed 1944	R 3 43	4 07	16 20	8 04	22 36	
14	Tu	Paris captured 1940	S20 18	4 47	16 57	9 16	23 01	
15	W	Mandela sentenced 1964	R 3 42	5 27	17 36	10 29	23 25	
16	Th	Enoch Powell b. 1922	S20 19	6 12	18 21	11 44	23 48	
17	F	Iceland independent 1944	R 3 42	7 04	19 17	13 01	—	
18	S	Waterloo Day	S20 20	8 11	20 29	14 20	0 13	
19	�	3rd Sunday after Trinity	R 3 42	9 25	21 49	15 40	0 42	
20	M	Wendy Craig b. 1934	S20 21	10 38	23 02	16 59	1 15	
21	Tu	Prince William b. 1982	R 3 43	11 44	—	18 13	1 57	
22	W	Judy Garland d. 1969	S20 21	0 08	12 42	19 17	2 48	
23	Th	Edward VIII b. 1894	R 3 43	1 06	13 34	20 11	3 50	
24	F	Midsummer Day	S20 21	1 58	14 22	20 53	5 00	
25	S	Korean War began 1950	R 3 44	2 46	15 07	21 27	6 14	
26	�	4th Sunday after Trinity	S20 21	3 32	15 49	21 55	7 28	
27	M	Joseph Smith killed 1844	R 3 45	4 17	16 31	22 19	8 41	
28	Tu	Sarajevo assass'ns 1914	S20 21	4 59	17 11	22 40	9 52	
29	W	AA formed 1905	R 3 46	5 42	17 51	23 01	11 00	
30	Th	Tower Bridge op. 1894	S20 21	6 24	18 34	23 22	12 06	

A somewhat cool and showry start to the month, but will become warm and sunny again with temperatures in the 70s.

MOON'S PHASES JUNE 1994		Days	Hrs.	Mins.
☾	Last Quarter	1	4	2
●	New Moon	9	8	26
☽	First Quarter	16	19	57
○	Full Moon	23	11	33
☾	Last Quarter	30	19	31

All times on this page are GMT (Add 1hr BST)

PREDICTIONS

The New Moon on the 9th falls in Gemini in a degree very important for nuclear energy, suggesting an important non-proliferation treaty, but also the risks of an accident. In the UK, the Government majority in the House of Commons will be threatened. The House of Lords will be flexing its muscles and the Labour Party will begin reorganising its constitution. In Russia there will be changes in the government, and possibly a change of leader. German troops will be in offensive action abroad. The US will be supremely confident and enforcing its global Pax Americana. In the Middle East religious militancy will be hitting a new peak, in response to increasing chances of an Israeli-Palestinian settlement. In Israel there will be a rising tide of popular protest over the latest peace plans. Instability in Iran will intensify whilst in Cyprus governmental changes will speed moves towards reunification between Turkish and Christian zones. *The Full Moon on the 23rd falls at the beginning of Capricorn.* It exactly opposes the eclipse at the birth of Prince William, indicating the possibility of changes in the succession. There will be a further leadership reshuffle in Russia.

The Epsom Derby may be won by the second favourite, and the Oaks by the favourite.

OLD MOORE'S predictions are world famous

Predicted German Reunification 1990

JULY

For High Water add, for Bristol 5h. 30m., Hull 4h. 23m., Leith 0h. 43m., and for Dublin sub. 2h. 21m., Greenock 1h. 22m., Liverpool 2h. 29m.

D of M	D of W	Sundays, Festivals Special Events, etc, for 1994	Sun Rises R Sets S	High Water at London Bridge Morn.	After.	Moon at London Rises	Sets	Wea- ther
			h. m.	h. m.	h. m.	h. m.	h. m.	
1	F	Princess of Wales b. 1961	R 3 47	7 10	19 23	23 44	13 11	
2	S	B. of Marston Moor 1644	S20 20	8 05	20 22	—	14 16	
3	☉	5th Sunday after Trinity	R 3 48	9 05	21 28	0 09	15 19	
4	M	US Independence Day	S20 19	10 10	22 37	0 38	16 20	
5	Tu	Georgette Heyer d. 1974	R 3 50	11 13	23 40	1 12	17 18	
6	W	Malawi independent 1964	S20 18	—	12 07	1 53	18 11	
7	Th	Dame Flora Robson d. 1984	R 3 52	0 29	12 50	2 43	18 57	
8	F	Vivien Leigh d. 1967	S20 17	1 12	13 33	3 40	19 38	
9	S	Civ. gas masks issue 1938	R 3 54	1 54	14 12	4 44	20 12	
10	☉	6th Sunday after Trinity	S20 16	2 34	14 53	5 53	20 41	
11	M	Yul Brynner b. 1916	R 3 56	3 14	15 31	7 05	21 07	
12	Tu	Bank Holiday (NI)	S20 14	3 53	16 06	8 19	21 31	
13	W	Harrison Ford b. 1942	R 3 58	4 31	16 42	9 34	21 55	
14	Th	National day of France	S20 12	5 11	17 20	10 50	22 19	
15	F	St Swithun's Day	R 4 00	5 53	18 01	12 07	22 46	
16	S	The hegira 622	S20 10	6 41	18 53	13 25	23 17	
17	☉	7th Sunday after Trinity	R 4 02	7 41	20 01	14 42	23 54	
18	M	Papal infallibility 1870	S20 08	8 54	21 22	15 56	—	
19	Tu	Simon Cadell b. 1950	R 4 05	10 10	22 42	17 03	0 39	
20	W	St Margaret	S20 06	11 23	23 57	18 00	1 35	
21	Th	Jonathan Miller b. 1934	R 4 08	—	12 28	18 47	2 39	
22	F	Wiliam Spooner b. 1844	S20 03	0 57	13 23	19 24	3 51	
23	S	National day of Ethiopia	R 4 10	1 49	14 09	19 55	5 05	
24	☉	8th Sunday after Trinity	S20 00	2 36	14 51	20 21	6 19	
25	M	Walter Brennan b. 1894	R 4 13	3 18	15 31	20 44	7 32	
26	Tu	Aldus Huxley b. 1894	S19 58	3 57	16 09	21 05	8 42	
27	W	James Mason d. 1984	R 4 16	4 35	16 44	21 26	9 50	
28	Th	Robespierre exec'd 1794	S19 55	5 11	17 19	21 48	10 56	
29	F	Drake played bowls 1588	R 4 19	5 47	17 56	22 12	12 01	
30	S	1st World Cup final 1930	S19 52	6 27	18 39	22 39	13 05	
31	☉	9th Sunday after Trinity	R 4 22	7 13	19 33	23 11	14 07	

The hottest month of the summer month heavy spells of rain and thundery intervals will occur. Towards the end of the 80s. with temperatures inthe 80s.

MOON'S PHASES JULY 1994

		Days	Hrs.	Mins.
●	New Moon	8	21	37
☽	First Quarter	16	1	12
○	Full Moon	22	20	16
☾	Last Quarter	30	12	40

All times on this page are GMT (Add 1hr BST)

PREDICTIONS

The New Moon on the 8th falls in Cancer, in a conjunction with the United Kingdom's Moon. Mars is square Saturn and Venus is square Pluto. This is a time when impulsive behaviour is all too likely to lead to accidents and blunders, and extreme caution is therefore necessary. In the UK the government should be strong and the opposition weak. There will be continued doubts over Britain's long-term role within the European community, but the main issue of the day will be social, including moves on penal reform, health care, including new provisions for the latest specialist treatment, and womens' rights at work, including provisions for maternity leave and child care. The leadership of the Liberal Democrats is likely to be subject to serious attack. There will be strikes in China and demonstrations or popular protests in Algeria. *The Full Moon on the 22nd will fall in Capricorn in an exact opposition to the Moon* for the independence of India and Pakistan, indicating popular excitement and demonstrations in both countries. In the UK the Scottish Nationalists will be enjoying a popular period and established parties on the defensive, as Nationalism thrives.

At Goodwood races the Stewards Cup may be won by the second favourite. Favourites should be noted in the non-handicaps.

1995 OLD MOORE on sale July 1994

Predicted the ATOM BOMB on HIROSHIMA, August 1945

Family Values Collapse

INSTABILITY

Saudi Arabian Threats

AUGUST

For High Water add, for Bristol 5h. 30m., Hull 4h. 23m., Leith 0h. 43m., and for Dublin sub. 2h. 21m., Greenock 1h. 22m., Liverpool 2h. 29m.

D of M	D of W	Sundays, Festivals Special Events, etc, for 1994	Sun Rises R Sets S	High Water at London Bridge Morn.	High Water at London Bridge After.	Moon at London Rises	Moon at London Sets	Weather
			h. m.	h. m.	h. m.	h. m.	h. m.	
1	M	Bank Holiday (Scotland)	S19 48	8 09	20 36	23 49	15 06	
2	Tu	Death duties introd. 1894	R 4 25	9 11	21 42	—	16 01	
3	W	Colette d. 1954	S19 45	10 16	22 52	0 35	16 50	
4	Th	Queen Mother b. 1900	R 4 28	11 25	23 57	1 28	17 33	
5	F	Richard Burton d. 1984	S19 42	—	12 22	2 30	18 11	
6	S	Anne Hathaway d. 1623	R 4 31	0 48	13 09	3 37	18 43	At first changeable conditions but it will bring warm and sunny with temperatures reaching the high 70s. Again, the occasional thunderstorm will prevail.
7	�	11th Sunday after Trinity	S19 38	1 33	13 52	4 49	19 11	
8	M	Nigel Mansell b. 1954	R 4 34	2 13	14 32	6 04	19 36	
9	Tu	Gerald Ford sworn in 1974	S19 35	2 54	15 10	7 20	20 01	
10	W	National day of Ecuador	R 4 37	3 34	15 46	8 37	20 25	
11	Th	Atlantic Charter 1941	S19 31	4 12	16 24	9 55	20 52	
12	F	Ian Fleming d. 1964	R 4 40	4 51	17 02	11 13	21 21	
13	S	Rod Hull b. 1935	S19 27	5 33	17 44	12 31	21 56	
14	�	11th Sunday after Trinity	R 4 43	6 18	18 35	13 45	22 38	
15	M	Princess Royal b. 1950	S19 23	7 16	19 42	14 53	23 29	
16	Tu	Peterloo Massacre 1819	R 4 47	8 26	21 03	15 52	—	
17	W	Ebor Handicap	S19 19	9 45	22 27	16 42	0 29	
18	Th	SA Olympics ban 1964	R 4 50	11 05	23 44	17 22	1 36	
19	F	Sir Henry Wood d. 1944	S19 15	—	12 14	17 55	2 48	
20	S	Jim Reeves b. 1924	R 4 53	0 46	13 09	18 23	4 00	
21	�	12th Sunday after Trinity	S19 11	1 37	13 54	18 47	5 13	
22	M	St Timothy	R 4 56	2 20	14 33	19 09	6 24	
23	Tu	Paris liberated 1944	S19 07	2 58	15 10	19 31	7 33	
24	W	St Bart's Day mass. 1572	R 4 59	3 34	15 43	19 52	8 40	
25	Th	James Watt d. 1819	S19 02	4 06	16 14	20 16	9 46	
26	F	Charles Lindbergh d. 1974	R 5 02	4 37	16 45	20 42	10 50	
27	S	Mother Teresa b. 1910	S18 58	5 09	17 20	21 12	11 53	
28	�	13th Sunday after Trinity	R 5 06	5 44	18 00	21 47	12 53	
29	M	Bank Holiday (except Scot.)	S18 54	6 24	18 45	22 29	13 49	
30	Tu	Cleopatra's suicide 30 BC	R 5 09	7 12	19 41	23 18	14 41	
31	W	Hallowe'en	S18 49	8 12	20 50	—	15 26	

MOON'S PHASES AUGUST 1994			Days	Hrs.	Mins.
	●	New Moon	7	8	45
	☽	First Quarter	14	5	57
	○	Full Moon	21	6	47
	☾	Last Quarter	29	6	41

All times on this page are GMT (Add 1 hr BST)

PREDICTIONS

The New Moon on the 7th falls in Leo. Jupiter in the second house is square to the New Moon and trine to Saturn, indicating rising economic confidence. It is unlikely that inflation will be contained, but will be seen as a price worth paying for improving economic activity. In the UK there could be a new fashion craze, but also much concern about the collapse of family values. The Indian sub-continent will be the focal point of instability, with changes of government likely in both India and Pakistan. Worldwide there should be strong pro-environment and pollution control measures. *The Full Moon on the 21st falls in a square to Pluto and an opposition to Regulus, the Royal star,* indicating rising public concern over what exactly the Monarch's job should be. There is a threat of leaks concerning Royal secrets, but the Queen would be advised to head off public criticism by making a charitable gesture. The Scottish Nationalists' popularity continues to grow. In the Middle East Saudi Arabia may threaten one of its neighbours, Egypt will be under increasing pressure from the fundamentalists, but a new, and possibly final, session of Israeli-Palestinian negotiations could begin.

At York races the Ebor Handicap may be won by a 4-y-o carrying 8st 4lbs and the Great Voltigeur Stakes by the favourite.

OLD MOORE is in "The Guinness Book of Records"

Predicted the abdication of King Edward VIII, 1936

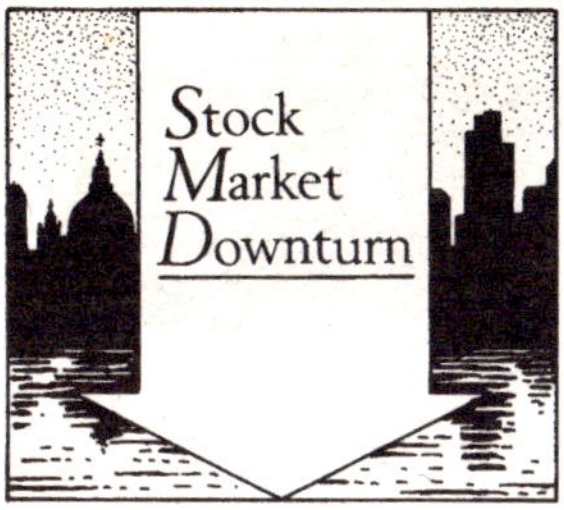

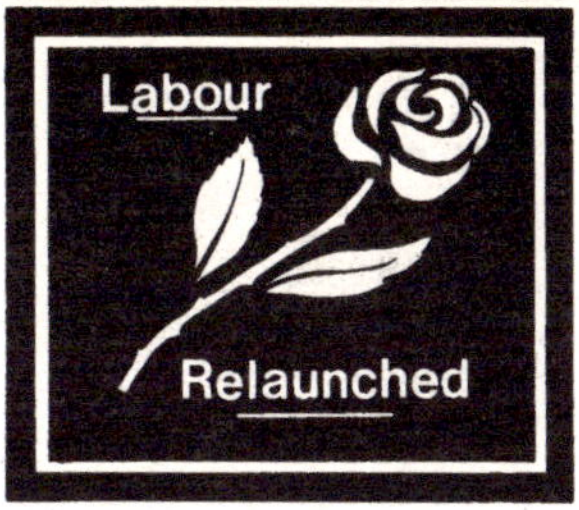

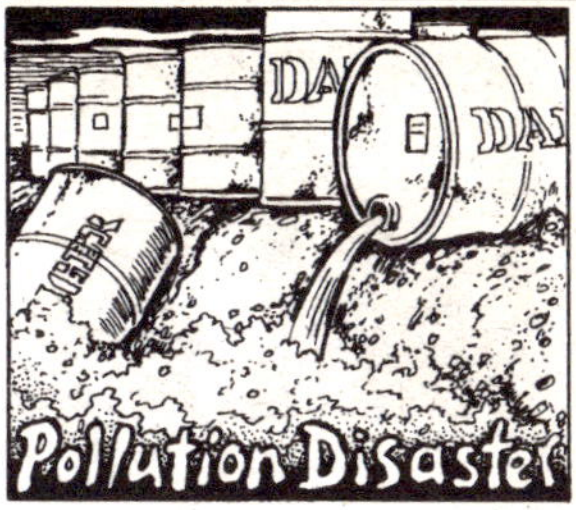

SEPTEMBER

For High Water add, for Bristol 5h. 30m., Hull 4h. 23m., Leith 0h. 43m., and for Dublin sub. 2h. 21m., Greenock 1h. 22m., Liverpool 2h. 29m.

D of M	D of W	Sundays, Festivals Special Events, etc, for 1994	Sun Rises R Sets S	High Water at London Bridge Morn.	High Water at London Bridge After.	Moon at London Rises	Moon at London Sets	Weather
			h. m.	h. m.	h. m.	h. m.	h. m.	
1	Th	St Giles	R 5 12	9 25	22 07	0 15	16 06	There's every chance of an Indian Summer with temperatures occasionally close to 70°F. Autumnal gales around mid-month will be followed by cooler weather.
2	F	B. of Sedan ended 1870	S18 45	10 44	23 22	1 19	16 40	
3	S	Pauline Collins b. 1940	R 5 15	11 51	—	2 28	17 10	
4	𝔖	14th Sunday after Trinity	S18 40	0 19	12 42	3 42	17 37	
5	M	Douglas Bader d. 1982	R 5 18	1 06	13 26	4 58	18 03	
6	Tu	Jewish New Year (5755)	S18 36	1 49	14 06	6 17	18 28	
7	W	Keith Moon d. 1978	R 5 22	2 30	14 46	7 36	18 55	
8	Th	First V-2 landed 1944	S18 31	3 10	15 24	8 57	19 24	
9	F	Flodden Field 1513	R 5 25	3 49	16 03	10 17	19 58	
10	S	St Leger, Doncaster	S18 27	4 30	16 45	11 34	20 39	
11	𝔖	15th Sunday after Trinity	R 5 28	5 13	17 30	12 45	21 27	
12	M	Steve Biko d. 1977	S18 22	6 00	18 24	13 47	22 24	
13	Tu	J.B. Priestley b. 1894	R 5 31	6 56	19 30	14 39	23 29	
14	W	Peace of Adrianople 1829	S18 18	8 04	20 47	15 22	—	
15	Th	Yom Kippur	R 5 34	9 21	22 10	15 56	0 38	
16	F	Lauren Bacall b. 1924	S18 13	10 44	23 27	16 25	1 49	
17	S	B. of Arnem began 1944	R 5 38	11 54	—	16 50	3 00	
18	𝔖	16th Sunday after Trinity	S18 08	0 28	12 49	17 13	4 10	
19	M	J. Péron overthrown 1955	R 5 41	1 17	13 33	17 35	5 18	
20	Tu	First day of Tabernacles	S18 04	1 58	14 12	17 57	6 26	
21	W	Malta independent 1964	R 5 44	2 34	14 46	18 19	7 32	
22	Th	Anne of Cleves b. 1515	S17 59	3 07	15 15	18 45	8 37	
23	F	J. Péron re-elected 1973	R 5 47	3 36	15 45	19 13	9 41	
24	S	*The Robe* première 1953	S17 54	4 03	16 14	19 46	10 42	
25	𝔖	17th Sunday after Trinity	R 5 50	4 33	16 48	20 25	11 39	
26	M	Battle of Arnem end 1944	S17 50	5 06	17 26	21 11	12 32	
27	Tu	St Damian	R 5 54	5 43	18 08	22 04	13 19	
28	W	Harpo Marx d. 1964	S17 45	6 25	18 57	23 03	14 00	
29	Th	Michaelmas	R 5 57	7 17	19 59	—	14 36	
30	F	Truman Capote b. 1924	S17 41	8 27	21 22	0 09	15 07	

MOON'S PHASES SEPTEMBER 1994

		Days	*Hrs.*	*Mins.*
●	New Moon	5	18	33
☽	First Quarter	12	11	34
○	Full Moon	19	20	1
☾	Last Quarter	28	0	23

All times on this page are GMT (Add 1hr BST)

PREDICTIONS

The New Moon on the 5th falls in Virgo in an opposition to Saturn indicating an atmosphere of 'business as usual'. Practicality and pragmatism will dominate world events. On the 1st the Sun, the Moon, Mars, Jupiter and Saturn will occupy an exact alignment which indicates a rapid speeding up in the pace of international events. This should be the financial turning point of the year, with stock markets experiencing a downturn through the autumn. However, there are still indications of a boom in the USA. In the UK there will be further talk of government reform, especially of widespread changes in local government. The Labour Party will be relaunched in a new, democratic form, whilst the Liberal Democrats will be experiencing an economic crisis. Expect changes of leadership in France and Germany. Russia's expansive mood will continue and in Asia and China will be asserting itself as the economic leader. In the Middle East there is a chance of revolution in Iraq and a peace deal in Israel. There may also be a change of government in Algeria. *The Full Moon on the 19th falls in Pisces conjunct the star Scheat,* indicating that many well-meaning ventures are set to flounder or sink without trace. There will be a major pollution disaster, possibly an oil leak.

At Doncaster races the St.Leger may be won by the favourite.

1995 RAPHAEL'S ALMANAC on sale September 1994

Predicted death of Yuri Andropov 1984

OCTOBER

For High Water add, for Bristol 5h. 30m., Hull 4h. 23m.,
Leith 0h. 43m., and for Dublin sub. 2h. 21m.,
Greenock 1h. 22m., Liverpool 2h. 29m.

D of M	D of W	Sundays, Festivals Special Events, etc, for 1994	Sun Rises R Sets S	High Water at London Bridge Morn.	After.	Moon at London Rises	Sets	Weather
			h. m.	h. m.	h. m.	h. m.	h. m.	
1	S	Watergate trial b'n 1974	R 6 00	9 59	22 42	1 19	15 35	Generally a pleasant start with some mild and sunny days, but it will get colder with strong winds and showers later in the month.
2	☽	18th Sunday after Trinity	S17 36	11 13	23 46	2 32	16 01	
3	M	Eddie Cochran b. 1938	R 6 03	—	12 08	3 49	16 27	
4	Tu	Charlton Heston b. 1924	S17 32	0 38	12 56	5 09	16 53	
5	W	Bob Geldof b. 1954	R 6 07	1 23	13 38	6 30	17 22	
6	Th	W.H. Smith d. 1891	S17 27	2 05	14 19	7 53	17 55	
7	F	Desmond Tutu b. 1931	R 6 10	2 46	15 01	9 14	18 35	
8	S	Rouben Mamoulian b. 1898	S17 23	3 28	15 45	10 30	19 22	
9	☽	19th Sunday after Trinity	R 6 13	4 10	16 31	11 38	20 18	
10	M	Eddie Cantor d. 1964	S17 18	4 57	17 20	12 35	21 21	
11	Tu	H.J. Heinz b. 1844	R 6 17	5 46	18 17	13 21	22 30	
12	W	Angela Rippon b. 1944	S17 14	6 39	19 19	13 58	23 41	
13	Th	Baroness Thatcher b. 1925	R 6 20	7 42	20 27	14 29	—	
14	F	Cliff Richard b. 1940	S17 10	8 53	21 46	14 55	0 51	
15	S	Khrushchev deposed 1964	R 6 23	10 16	23 04	15 18	2 01	
16	☽	20th Sunday after Trinity	S17 05	11 29	—	15 40	3 09	
17	M	St Etheldreda	R 6 27	0 04	12 24	16 01	4 16	
18	Tu	'Beau' Nash b. 1674	S17 01	0 52	13 09	16 24	5 22	
19	W	B. of Cedar Creek 1864	R 6 30	1 34	13 47	16 48	6 27	
20	Th	Dame Anna Neagle b. 1904	S16 57	2 08	14 19	17 15	7 30	
21	F	Trafalgar Day	R 6 34	2 39	14 49	17 47	8 32	
22	S	Joan Fontaine b. 1917	S16 53	3 05	15 17	18 24	9 31	
23	☽	21st Sunday after Trinity	R 6 37	3 32	15 48	19 07	10 25	
24	M	Jack Warner b. 1894	S16 49	4 03	16 23	19 56	11 14	
25	Tu	St Crispin	R 6 41	4 37	17 01	20 53	11 57	
26	W	William Temple d. 1944	S16 45	5 13	17 42	21 54	12 34	
27	Th	Dylan Thomas b. 1914	R 6 44	5 53	18 27	23 01	13 06	
28	F	Robert Liston b. 1794	S16 41	6 41	19 24	—	13 34	
29	S	National day of Turkey	R 6 48	7 42	20 39	0 10	14 01	
30	☽	22nd Sunday after Trinity	S16 37	9 08	22 02	1 23	14 26	
31	M	Indira Gandhi assass. 1984	R 6 51	10 30	23 11	2 40	14 51	

MOON'S PHASES OCTOBER 1994

		Days	Hrs.	Mins.
●	New Moon	5	3	55
☽	First Quarter	11	19	17
○	Full Moon	19	12	18
☾	Last Quarter	27	16	44

All times GMT (BST to Oct 23 + 1hr)

PREDICTIONS

The New Moon on the 5th falls in Libra bringing confidence to the UK. Britain will be infected by economic hysteria, the belief in economic recovery and signs of a high street boom. Even in the House of Commons there are likely to be rare scenes of emotion and enthusiasm. Internationally, optimism is likely to lead to hopes of breakthrough in the quest for peace in a range of international conflicts. However, the window of opportunity is very slight, and prospects for peace radically worsen after the middle of the month. There are likely to be changes in the leadership of the Conservative Party. Russia will be moving sharply towards increased nationalism and intervention in other countries. In Japan a period of political instability is beginning which will last into 1995. Military and revolutionary instability in both Iran and Iraq indicates no end to disturbance in the Gulf. *The Full Moon on the 19th falls in Aries in a square to Uranus and Neptune,* indicating a rapid slide to international misunderstanding and conflict. In Europe, NATO will by now be effectively reconstituted into a European army, including Russian troops.

At Newmarket races the Cambridgeshire may be won by a 6-y-o carrying 9st 2lbs and the Cesarewitch by a 4-y-o carrying 7st 10lbs.

Clocks back 1 hour, 23 October

Predicted resignation of Margaret Thatcher 1990

NOVEMBER

For High Water add, for Bristol 5h. 30m., Hull 4h. 23m.,
Leith 0h. 43m., and for Dublin sub. 2h. 21m.,
Greenock 1h. 22m., Liverpool 2h. 29m.

D of M	D of W	Sundays, Festivals Special Events, etc, for 1994	Sun Rises R Sets S	High Water at London Bridge Morn.	High Water at London Bridge After.	Moon at London Rises	Moon at London Sets	Weather
			h. m.	h. m.	h. m.	h. m.	h. m.	
1	Tu	M1 opened 1959	S16 34	11 33	—	3 59	15 18	
2	W	Ken Rosewall b. 1934	R 6 55	0 07	12 25	5 20	15 49	
3	Th	Henri Matisse d. 1954	S16 30	0 56	13 13	6 43	16 25	
4	F	Loretta Swit b. 1944	R 6 58	1 41	13 58	8 04	17 10	
5	S	Gunpowder Plot 1605	S16 27	2 25	14 43	9 19	18 03	
6	☾	23rd Sunday after Trinity	R 7 02	3 08	15 31	10 23	19 06	
7	M	Lord Lucan vanished 1974	S16 23	3 55	16 20	11 16	20 16	
8	Tu	Margaret Mitchell b. 1900	R 7 05	4 42	17 11	11 57	21 28	
9	W	Hedy Lamarr b. 1913	S16 20	5 32	18 04	12 31	22 41	
10	Th	Tim Rice b. 1944	R 7 09	6 22	19 00	12 59	23 52	
11	F	Home Guard disband 1944	S16 17	7 17	20 01	13 23	—	
12	S	Lord Mayor's Show	R 7 12	8 20	21 11	13 45	1 00	
13	☾	Remembrance Sunday	S16 14	9 36	22 28	14 07	2 07	
14	M	Prince of Wales b. 1948	R 7 16	10 55	23 33	14 29	3 13	
15	Tu	Petula Clark b. 1934	S16 11	11 54	—	14 52	4 18	
16	W	Murray R. discov'd 1824	R 7 19	0 24	12 41	15 18	5 22	
17	Th	St Hilda	S16 08	1 04	13 20	15 48	6 24	
18	F	Emperor Vespasian b. 9	R 7 23	1 41	13 54	16 23	7 24	
19	S	Jaqueline du Pré d. 1987	S16 06	2 11	14 25	17 04	8 20	
20	☾	25th Sunday after Trinity	R 7 26	2 40	14 56	17 52	9 11	
21	M	Voltaire b. 1694	S16 04	3 10	15 29	18 46	9 56	
22	Tu	Arthur Eddington d. 1944	R 7 29	3 43	16 06	19 46	10 35	
23	W	St Clement	S16 01	4 17	16 42	20 49	11 08	
24	Th	Thanksgiving (US)	R 7 32	4 54	17 22	21 56	11 37	
25	F	Imran Khan b. 1952	S16 00	5 32	18 05	23 06	12 03	
26	S	Tina Turner b. 1939	R 7 36	6 14	18 56	—	12 28	
27	☾	1st Sunday in Advent	S15 58	7 09	20 02	0 18	12 52	
28	M	Sinn Fein founded 1905	R 7 39	8 23	21 21	1 33	13 17	
29	Tu	Sir George Robey d. 1954	S15 56	9 46	22 34	2 51	13 44	
30	W	St Andrew's Day	R 7 42	10 58	23 37	4 11	14 16	

Another reasonably mild and sunny start until mid-month when the first frosts of winter and the odd snowfall will create a sharp drop in temperature.

MOON'S PHASES NOVEMBER 1994

		Days	Hrs.	Mins.
●	New Moon	3	13	36
☽	First Quarter	10	6	14
○	Full Moon	18	6	57
☾	Last Quarter	26	7	4

All times on this page are GMT

PREDICTIONS

The New Moon on the 3rd is an eclipse and falls in Scorpio conjunct Venus and trine Saturn, indicating positive moves towards peace and reconstruction. However, other indications are that such moves will be necessary in order to stem the rising tide of international conflict. The British economy will be growing, but pessimists will warn that it is about to overheat. The Liberal Democrats will be in a very strong position. China will be flexing its muscles by initiating international economic conflicts, and both Iraq and Pakistan may experience continuing instability. *The Full Moon on the 18th is an eclipse in Taurus, is opposed Pluto, square Mars and conjunct the star Caput Algol.* There is now a maximum risk of random violence and terrorism, including that sponsored by governments. The Balkans are approaching a last major wave of instability, which could draw in other countries in the east, such as the Ukraine. In the US there is a major risk of serious riots. Both the British Conservative Party and the Monarchy will be coming to the end of three years of trauma, perhaps with one final battle. In Israel there is a serious chance of Palestinian autonomy.

At Doncaster races the November Handicap may be won by a horse carrying 8st 13lbs.

Horse Racing Forecasts, pages 67/69

News of the Future in MOORE'S ALMANACK

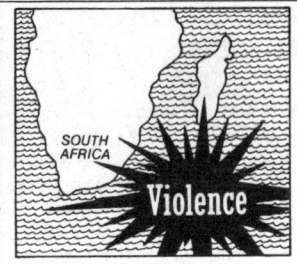

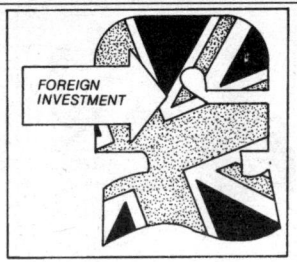

DECEMBER

For High Water add, for Bristol 5h. 30m., Hull 4h. 23m., Leith 0h. 43m., and for Dublin sub. 2h. 21m., Greenock 1h. 22m., Liverpool 2h. 29m.

D of M	D of W	Sundays, Festivals Special Events, etc, for 1994	Sun Rises R Sets S	High Water at London Bridge Morn.	High Water at London Bridge After.	Moon at London Rises	Moon at London Sets	Wea-ther
			h. m.	h. m.	h. m.	h. m.	h. m.	
1	Th	Queen Alexandra b. 1844	S15 55	11 58	—	5 32	14 56	
2	F	G. Mercator d. 1594	R 7 44	0 32	12 52	6 50	15 44	
3	S	R.L. Stevenson d. 1894	S15 54	1 23	13 42	8 02	16 43	
4	�	2nd Sunday in Advent	R 7 47	2 09	14 32	9 02	17 51	
5	M	*Marie Celeste* found 1872	S15 53	2 56	15 19	9 51	19 06	
6	Tu	Cyril Washbrook b. 1914	R 7 50	3 42	16 09	10 29	20 21	
7	W	F. de Lesseps d. 1894	S15 52	4 28	16 58	11 01	21 35	
8	Th	James Thurber b. 1894	R 7 52	5 15	17 47	11 27	22 47	
9	F	Elis. Schwarzkopf b. 1915	S15 51	6 00	18 36	11 51	23 56	
10	S	Dan Maskell d. 1992	R 7 54	6 49	19 28	12 13	—	
11	�	3rd Sunday in Advent	S15 51	7 42	20 29	12 34	1 03	
12	M	Connie Francis b. 1938	R 7 56	8 47	21 39	12 57	2 09	
13	Tu	B. of R. Plate b' 1939	S15 51	10 04	22 52	13 22	3 13	
14	W	Andrei Sakharov d. 1989	R 7 58	11 18	23 49	13 50	4 16	
15	Th	Sitting Bull killed 1890	S15 51	—	12 10	14 23	5 17	
16	F	B. of the Bulge began 1944	R 8 00	0 35	12 53	15 02	6 14	
17	S	*Graf Spee* scuttled 1939	S15 52	1 13	13 30	15 48	7 07	
18	�	4th Sunday in Advent	R 8 01	1 47	14 04	16 40	7 55	
19	M	Linoleum patent 1863	S15 52	2 19	14 39	17 38	8 36	
20	Tu	Artur Rubinstein d. 1982	R 8 03	2 54	15 15	18 41	9 11	
21	W	St Thomas the Apostle	S15 53	3 29	15 52	19 47	9 42	
22	Th	Dreyfus imprisoned 1894	R 8 04	4 04	16 30	20 56	10 09	
23	F	Emperor Akihito b. 1933	S15 54	4 40	17 06	22 06	10 34	
24	S	Christmas Eve	R 8 05	5 15	17 47	23 18	10 57	
25	�	Christmas Day	S15 55	5 54	18 32	—	11 21	
26	M	Boxing Day	R 8 05	6 41	19 30	0 32	11 46	
27	Tu	Holiday	S15 57	7 45	20 43	1 48	12 15	
28	W	Mary II d. 1694	R 8 06	9 07	21 59	3 06	12 49	
29	Th	Coelocanth caught 1952	S15 58	10 26	23 11	4 23	13 31	
30	F	Amelia Bloomer d. 1894	R 8 06	11 37	—	5 37	14 22	
31	S	New Year's Eve	S16 00	0 14	12 39	6 42	15 25	

Generally a cold month with wintry conditions and the occasional snow shower, but the chances of a White Christmas are remote.

MOON'S PHASES DECEMBER 1994

		Days	Hrs.	Mins.
●	New Moon	2	23	54
☽	First Quarter	9	21	6
○	Full Moon	18	2	17
☾	Last Quarter	25	19	6

All times on this page are GMT

PREDICTIONS

The New Moon on the 2nd falls in Pisces, is square to Saturn and exactly on the IC. at London. Mars square to Jupiter and Pluto maintains a level of international irrationality and belligerence, with the Balkans remaining one of the most unstable trouble spots. In Israel, a long threatening period is now almost at an end, and will be finally over by late 1995, and all attempts should be made to see that agreements with the Arabs are genuine and long-lasting. In North Africa the continuing destabilising pressure will be felt most in Algeria, where there will be changes in the leadership. In South Africa there is the profound threat of a sudden outburst of violence. In the UK the opposition will be very strong, and there are likely to be strikes either in the schools, transport or postal services. Steps should be taken to safeguard against all transport accidents. *The Full Moon on the 18th falls in Gemini. Mars, Jupiter and Saturn are in square and opposition to each other* indicating serious possibilities for recovery and reconstruction. In the UK there could be widespread financial restructuring, with news of extensive foreign investment. In Japan political instability will deepen and public unrest is a possibility.

The King George VI Chase at Kempton may be won by the favourite.

OLD MOORE for all the family

Cont'd from p. 33

LEO BORN PEOPLE

OCTOBER INFLUENCES: 1-2nd Contacts from the past occur in your life again and bring some surprises. 16-17th Finances begin to strengthen after a period of slight austerity. 30-31st An excellent end to the month, but don't be side-tracked from your personal objectives. OPPORTUNITIES: 28-29th A period when telling the truth as you see it can only work to your advantage. LIMITING INFLUENCES: 13-14th Try and greet life with a smile, even though others are less likely to do so at present.

NOVEMBER INFLUENCES: 1-2nd Emotionally speaking you should be on top form and able to deal with anything. 20-21st Boring routines are unlikely to prevent you from making general progress. 29-30th It's all too easy to dodge issues right now, but gains come from facing up to them. OPPORTUNITIES: 24-25th Take the chance to get out and about as much as proves to be possible. LIMITING INFLUENCES: 9-11th A period when some aspects of life look blacker than is really justified.

DECEMBER INFLUENCES: 1-2nd Minor disruptions to general routines are unlikely to last very long. 9-10th Most Leos find themselves to be especially brave at present. 27-29th Controversy follows you, but turns out to be part of your appeal just for the moment. OPPORTUNITIES: 21-22nd Your nature is appealing and especially attractive to almost everyone you meet. LIMITING INFLUENCES: 7-8th A quiet phase, not especially good for new plans and schemes, so take a little rest.

VIRGO BORN PEOPLE

Birthdays between August 24th and September 23rd inclusive. Your planet is Mercury. Birthstone, Sardonyx. Lucky day, Wednesday.

KEYNOTE FOR THE YEAR   There ought to be plenty to keep you occupied, though there are certain frustrations at the start of the year. Confidence peaks before the arrival of the Summer.

JANUARY INFLUENCES: 1-2nd Look to improving the quality of your personal life as much as possible. 9-10th Slower prospects, though advancement is still possible. 27-28th Conversations throw up some very interesting ideas. OPPORTUNITIES: 30-31st Confusion is ended in terms of personal relationships and what they have to offer you. LIMITING INFLUENCES: 15-16th A brave attitude to life does little to make things go the way that you would wish during this period.

FEBRUARY INFLUENCES: 3-4th Look for variety and freedom in almost everything that you are doing at present. A good time to take risk. 15-16th Less influential now but you are still able to talk others round to your way of thinking. 29-30th Relatives come good in helping to further your ideas. OPPORTUNITIES: 26-27th Routines are out and the chance of journey of some sort should not be dismissed. LIMITING INFLUENCES: 13-14th In your efforts to do everything at once you are almost certain to find that obstacles come along.

MARCH INFLUENCES: 1-2nd Not a bad start to the month but you will need to keep your options open as much as possible. 9-10th There are now many different ways of looking at things, so concentrate if you can. 28-29th As the end of the month approaches take stock of recent successes and keep trying. OPPORTUNITIES: 26-27th The more you believe in yourself, the better are the chances that most situations go your way. LIMITING INFLUENCES: 11-12th Prepare yourself for some minor struggles at work and rely instead on personal possibilities.

APRIL INFLUENCES: 4-5th A mysterious interlude, though one that definitely works to your advantage. 14-15th Mid-month considerations tend to make you feel content with the way that things are going. 25-26th Two almost perfect days for many Virgoans. Keep up the good work professionally. OPPORTUNITIES: 22-23rd You need to concentrate, and if you do all sorts of possibilities make for an interesting time. LIMITING INFLUENCES: 8-9th No matter how bold you try to be, other people are inclined to let you down.

VIRGO BORN PEOPLE

MAY INFLUENCES: 1-2nd A good start to the month of May, being productive and quite interesting personally speaking. 17-18th An unusual interlude, though one that is full of personal promise and also good luck. 27-28th Sporting ventures look like working out to your advantage, for a day or two at least. OPPORTUNITIES: 19-20th Prepare yourself for an extremely active and very rewarding period. LIMITING INFLUENCES: 5-6th If you are too regimented in the way that you look at life, don't be surprised to find that things go wrong.

JUNE INFLUENCES: 2-3rd Personal decisions are far more important than professional ones as the month gets off to a slightly frustrating start. 11-12th Keep up the good work in a practical sense and ignore the possibility of arguments at home. 30th If you want a perfect day, fall in line with the offers that are coming in all the time.OPPORTUNITIES: 15-16th Excellent prospects exist in a career sense and with regard to taking chances of one sort or another. LIMITING INFLUENCES: 28-29th Limited progress cash-wise.

JULY INFLUENCES: 4-5th There are some surprises about, simply keep your eyes open and make the best of them. 16-17th Mid-month blues are quickly blown away on the breeze of change. 30-31st End the month with a flourish and don't allow negative types to curb your enthusiasm. OPPORTUNITIES: 13-14th Confidence is all important at present and is not especially hard to come by. LIMITING INFLUENCES: 26-27th Keeping up with the Jones' is not something that you should be trying to do just for the moment.

AUGUST INFLUENCES: 1-2nd An easy going and friendly Virgoan greets the Summer weather and all the new possibilities. 17-18th Constant attention to detail will not do you any good, so look for change and diversity if you possibly can. 25-26th You warm easily to the needs that others have of you. OPPORTUNITIES: 9-10th Standard responses to others won't work. Be prepared to stick your neck out. LIMITING INFLUENCES: 22-23rd Not everyone has your best interests at heart right now.

SEPTEMBER INFLUENCES: 1-2nd A good period for deciding to get things done in and around the house, likewise for unexpected travel. 16-17th Events slow down, though only to give you time to make up your own mind more slowly. 25-26th Not easy to conform to expectations at present, but then why should you? OPPORTUNITIES: 5-6th No matter what you decide to take on, there is energy to spare right now. LIMITING INFLUENCES: 18-20th Reaction time is slow and you need hours alone to think.

OCTOBER INFLUENCES: 1-2nd Personalities crop up all the time in your life at present and you need the chance to shine socially. 12-13th A very cheerful Virgoan is on offer to the world at present, make the most of change. 29-30th Some confusion is more or less inevitable, though probably not for long. OPPORTUNITIES: 3-4th A better time than of late for spoiling yourself financially. Don't be held back. LIMITING INFLUENCES: 15-17th Although bright in yourself, others demand too much of you.

NOVEMBER INFLUENCES: 5-6th In some ways the most important days of the month, no matter how quiet they might seem. A time to plan. 16-17th Early confusion soon clears and leaves you feeling very fresh and active. 29-30th Finish the month by thinking about organising events for the festive season to come. OPPORTUNITIES: 27-28th At your chatty best you are able to make gains simply by opening your mouth. LIMITING INFLUENCES: 12-13th Rules and regulations could easily get on your nerves now.

DECEMBER INFLUENCES: 1-2nd Start December as you mean the month to go on, no time for half-hearted ventures. 17-18th Although plans for Christmas may change, they do so for the best. 30-31st An excellent time for laying down all the resolutions that you can think up. OPPORTUNITIES: 24-25th The Moon supports all your Christmas efforts and should make for a happy time. LIMITING INFLUENCES: 9-10th Cash could be in short supply, for the moment at least.

LIBRA BORN PEOPLE

**Birthdays between September 24th and October 23rd inclusive.
Your planet is Venus. Birthstone, opal. Lucky day, Friday.**

KEYNOTE FOR THE YEAR Confidence is all important at the start of the year, when you have the ability to make all sorts of situations turn out to your advantage. Romance and travel are important later in the year.

JANUARY INFLUENCES: 1-2nd There is much to be gained by channelling energy in the right directions. 11-12th Routines could be something of a chore but there are gains to be had as a result of concentration. 23-24th An adventurous streak finds you out there doing whatever takes your fancy. OPPORTUNITIES: 3-4th Build up your personal resources by being in the right place at the right time. LIMITING INFLUENCES: 16-17th People are more difficult to understand now and require some close scrutiny.

FEBRUARY INFLUENCES: 3-4th At this time you tend to wake up to a number of new possibilities that are on offer. 10th Take special care when dealing with deliberately awkward types of people. 22nd Continued reliance on friends is vitally important. 27-28th End the month by getting up to date with outstanding jobs. OPPORTUNITIES: 1-2nd Compliments come your way from a number of different and surprising directions. LIMITING INFLUENCES: 14-15th Restrictions could be placed upon your forward progress.

MARCH INFLUENCES: 1-2nd Emotional problems are less difficult to overcome at this time. 9-10th Congratulations could be in order somewhere within the family so keep your ears open. 26-27th Practical considerations are a little like walking a tightrope and great care is necessary in relationships. OPPORTUNITIES: 28-29th As long as you are bold and ambitious life works for you. LIMITING INFLUENCES: 13-14th Confidence tends to be low and support is lacking generally.

APRIL INFLUENCES: 4-5th You are very eager to express your ideas and should find a willing audience. 14-15th Personal doubts are soon dispelled as relationships begin to improve. 29-30th You seem to be looking at the possibility of renewed popularity when in the company of associates. OPPORTUNITIES: 24-25th Your own needs and wants now take priority over time spent on others. LIMITING INFLUENCES: 10-11th Relatives and friends alike are difficult to deal with for a couple of days, life is slow.

MAY INFLUENCES: 2-3rd If you are taking on new commitments you should do so in a considered and slow way. 14-15th Practical matters carry definite signposts for the future and offer many new incentives. 30-31st With the scent of summer in your nostrils you are able to wave some cares goodbye. OPPORTUNITIES: 21-22nd Decisive actions at this time will open the door for significant success to come. LIMITING INFLUENCES: 7-8th A wait and see attitude works better than trying to force things through.

JUNE INFLUENCES: 1-2nd All-round success is possible now, though not if you try to rush your fences. 7-8th Not everyone shares your opinions at present, though you should be able to talk them round. 26-27th Good career prospects, especially for those looking for a change. OPPORTUNITIES: 18-19th New friends are on the cards and some of them are useful as well as interesting. LIMITING INFLUENCES: 4-5th There are not many opportunities to make gains at this time.

JULY INFLUENCES: 3-4th Romantic problems hanging on from the past can now be rectified. 19-20th Continued success through most spheres of your life and especially in a career sense. 30-31st Not a time to be creeping around or for hiding your light under a bushel. OPPORTUNITIES: 15-16th You could be standing on the threshold of important new ventures practically speaking. LIMITING INFLUENCES: 28-29th It could appear that even your best friends fail to understand you are present.

. .52. .

LIBRA BORN PEOPLE

AUGUST INFLUENCES: 1-2nd It is important to start the month with great confidence, even if it is hard to find within yourself. 14-15th A combination of good luck and happy coincidences really do lift you at present. 29-30th There are surprises in store, not least of all in your love life. OPPORTUNITIES: 11-12th Personal attachments strengthen and leave you feeling quite secure. LIMITING INFLUENCES: 24-26th Outmoded concepts should be left behind once and for all.

SEPTEMBER INFLUENCES: 3-4th A sunny and happy time for most Librans and ideal for travel prospects.12-13th A period of high activity allow you the chance to catch your breath in a number of areas. 29-30th Not a startling end to the month, though there are personal advantages to be gained. OPPORTUNITIES: 8-9th If you ever take a chance financially, this period is for you. LIMITING INFLUENCES: 21-22nd It's possible that someone is trying to dupe you at present.

OCTOBER INFLUENCES: 3-4th Conversation proves interesting and you are in the right mood to make significant new contacts. 15-16th Mid-month worries tend to disappear like the morning mist if you refuse to take them seriously. 29-30th Make changes around the home now for more comfort in the colder weather that lies ahead. OPPORTUNITIES: 5-6th Even the most casual of conversations lead to new opportunities at this time. LIMITING INFLUENCES: 18-19th Those around you seem to be quite unfair in their behaviour.

NOVEMBER INFLUENCES: 5-6th Things quieten down a little, though gains can still be made slowly and steadily. 19-20th Not a time to be too quiet, people want to hear what you have to say. 29-30th Routines are a bore, though not if you are prepared to ring the changes. OPPORTUNITIES: 3-4th The best of times are possible and many of them out of the blue, take full advantage. LIMITING INFLUENCES: 15-16th It's not easy to go with the flow, especially when you disapprove.

DECEMBER INFLUENCES: 1-2nd A good start to the month, though prior-planning is very necessary. 17-18th Very busy on the run-up to Christmas, take some rest if you possibly can. 30-31st Some uncertainty at the end of the year is forgotten in the midst of all the fun. OPPORTUNITIES: 26-27th All practical aspects of life seem to be to the fore and bring benefits. LIMITING INFLUENCES: 11-12th People generally are not as helpful as you might wish and patience is necessary.

SCORPIO BORN PEOPLE

Birthdays between October 24th and November 22nd inclusive. Your planets are Mars and Pluto. Birthstone, topaz. Lucky day, Tuesday.

KEYNOTE FOR THE YEAR: A happy Scorpio greets the year, though you may notice a quiet spell in the Spring. Be bold in all personal matters.

JANUARY INFLUENCES: 1-2nd A slight slowing down of situations would be favourable at the start of the year. 12-13th Confidence is on the increase and so are advantages. 30-31st The attitudes of others are variable, though you seem to carry on regardless of them. OPPORTUNITIES: 5-6th Finances look as though they may strengthen though relationships may not. LIMITING INFLUENCES: 21-22nd Purpose is a little lacking from your daily life and more effort is required.

FEBRUARY INFLUENCES: 1-2nd The deeper and more home loving qualities of your nature are really shining out now. 15-16th A thoughtful and contemplative Scorpio is really on show at present. 25-26th You tend to adopt a high profile attitude to most situations. OPPORTUNITIES: 2-3rd A perfect time to think about changes in or around the home. LIMITING INFLUENCES: 17-18th No matter how hard you try, people may refuse to help you fulfil your objectives at present.

SCORPIO BORN PEOPLE

MARCH INFLUENCES: 4-5th Confidence comes flooding in to do whatever takes your fancy. 18-19th It looks as though you are in the mood for Spring, no matter what the weather is doing outside. 25-26th The slightly off-beat attitude of others could puzzle you at this time. OPPORTUNITIES: 1-2nd An excellent time to organise yourself and to get practicalities sorted out once and for all. LIMITING INFLUENCES: 16-17th You are apt to miss out on the last push that leads to success.

APRIL INFLUENCES: 1-2nd Variable prospects are on offer for the month, don't be put off by ignorant types. 17-18th Original ideas can be followed through and bring significant dividends. 28-29th There is no point in moaning about things that go wrong, simply pitch in and sort them out. OPPORTUNITIES: 26-27th Ambitions are well spotlighted right now and you can be certain that you are working to your best capabililites. LIMITING INFLUENCES: 13-14th Not everyone appears to have your best interests at heart.

MAY INFLUENCES: 1-2nd Although you don't lack energy at the start of the month, not everyone is backing you up. 15-16th Small successess now lead to much greater ones in the fullness of time. 29-30th A good friend seems to have a fairly serious attitude problem for the moment. OPPORTUNITIES: 23-24th Routines don't get you down and you can get through a thousand jobs at the same time. LIMITING INFLUENCES: 10-11th Confusion in personal relationships must be dealt with carefully.

JUNE INFLUENCES: 1-2nd A slightly more conservative phase starts the month, but won't stay around long. 9-10th Not everyone is easy to get on with but this should not be allowed to prevent your forward progress. 29-30th Many Scorpios can register the fact that they do not have a care in the world at present. OPPORTUNITIES: 20-21st You have great enthusiasm at this time and can easily get your own way in most things. LIMITING INFLUENCES: 6-7th Confidence to do the right thing is hard to come by now.

JULY INFLUENCES: 3-4th The lead-up to an interesting phase, get existing jobs out of the way quickly. 15-16th Itemise what has to be done at present and do your best to tackle things slowly and steadily. 27-28th Confidence should be high, though personal relationships need thinking through carefully. OPPORTUNITIES: 17-18th You appear to be on top form and the Moon is in an excellent position to be of assistance. LIMITING INFLUENCES: 4-5th Minimise problems by keeping yourself to yourself.

AUGUST INFLUENCES: 1-2nd Spend a little time thinking up ways to improve your personal comfort. 10-11th If you stand on the outside of situations you will fail to understand what is really going on. 20th Make time to get out and see friends. 29th Look towards a journey or some sort of impromptu outing. OPPORTUNITIES: 13-14th A search for security leads you down some interesting roads. LIMITING INFLUENCES: 27-28th Not everything that you would really want to do at present is as fortunate as you might hope.

SEPTEMBER INFLUENCES: 2-3rd Emotionally speaking your nature is supercharged as the month gets off to a flying start for most Scorpios. 15-16th Avoid the chance of jealousy getting in the way of happiness right now. 29-30th Be prepared for obstacles on the path towards greater self-choice. OPPORTUNITIES: 10-11th The best days of the month for pushing your projects into the spotlight. LIMITING INFLUENCES: 23-24th Practicalities have to take a back seat as you seek rest.

OCTOBER INFLUENCES: 1-2nd People are calling upon your strength of character at the start of the month, so be bold. 12-13th There are contradictions about in a personal sense and do need resolving. 25-26th Wait for a day or two before trying to put really grandiose schemes into action. OPPORTUNITIES: 7-8th Stick to the things that you know at present and it's possible to work wonders. LIMITING INFLUENCES: 20-22nd A few disappointments are inevitable, don't let them get you down.

SCORPIO BORN PEOPLE

NOVEMBER INFLUENCES: 1-2nd When good ideas come along, as they do right now, be certain to make a note of them for later. 19-20th You may sense the calm before a storm when it comes to domestic issues of one sort or another. 27-28th Try to avoid being over-anxious about details of any sort for a couple of days. OPPORTUNITIES: 3-4th You stand alone in the estimation of some fairly important people. LIMITING INFLUENCES: 17-18th A time to think about personal issues as carefully as you are able.

DECEMBER INFLUENCES: 4-5th You already have Christmas in your sights and should be planning carefully. 19-20th The last big push before the festive season. Stay cool in social situations. 30-31st Make certain that your resolutions for the new year are realistic and workable. OPPORTUNITIES: 1-2nd Significant financial possibilities surround you at this time. LIMITING INFLUENCES: 14-15th Problems press in an you may be a little fatigued.

SAGITTARIUS BORN PEOPLE

Birthdays between November 23rd and December 21st inclusive. Your planet is Jupiter. Birthstone, turquoise. Lucky day, Thursday.

KEYNOTE FOR THE YEAR   Considerable effort is put into expanding your horizons at the beginning of the year and you can reap the benefit of your efforts as the months go by. Be aware of romantic possibilities.

JANUARY INFLUENCES: 1-2nd A sensible start to the year, but perhaps just a little tedious. 15-16th Considering the feelings of those around you is important, but don't forget yourself. 30-31st The Winter ends in your mind, even if it still hasn't out of doors. OPPORTUNITIES: 7-8th A quality time for personal relationships and making new friends. LIMITING INFLUENCES: 22-23rd Some frustrations now are beyond your own control and you should rely more on the help of friends.

FEBRUARY INFLUENCES: 2-3rd An excellent start to the month, with great social prospects on offer. 16-17th Surprises are in store at present, though most of them should be of a pleasant nature. 27-28th Avoid personal confrontations that cannot help you out at all. OPPORTUNITIES: 5-6th Ask for favours from people who you have been able to help out in the past. LIMITING INFLUENCES: 19-21st Not a good period for saying the first thing that comes into your mind.

MARCH INFLUENCES: 1-2nd Not everyone you come across is as reliable as they may appear to be. 15-16th Steady progress is indicated but this is no time to take chances. 30-31st Better finances are on offer, though you will have to look for them. OPPORTUNITIES: 4-5th Your decision-making abilities are well highlighted at present so take a chance or two. LIMITING INFLUENCES: 19-20th Career prospects are apt to take a short nosedive, but don't over-react.

APRIL INFLUENCES: 2-3rd It is in the area of social mixing that you really begin to prosper at the start of this month. 19-20th Most of your conclusions are now based on sound thinking and plenty of experience. 26-27th Look out for some rather interesting possibilities in a financial sense. OPPORTUNITIES: 28-29th Security is more possible now and you are looking towards improvements at home. LIMITING INFLUENCES: 14-15th Much more quiet than normal, you need space to think things through.

. .58. .

SAGITTARIUS BORN PEOPLE

MAY INFLUENCES: 1-2nd Chance meetings prove to be especially lucky and to offer new incentives. 15-16th The world should seem full of wonders, if it doesn't you have your eyes shut now. 28-29th Stay away from situations that mean becoming involved in arguments you can't win. OPPORTUNITIES: 25-26th Dividends financially are complimented by significant popularity generally. LIMITING INFLUENCES: 12-14th Don't allow yourself to come under the influence of disreputable types.

JUNE INFLUENCES: 1-2nd You may be just a little too abrupt for your own good. 14-15th Times are good and there is the chance to do whatever takes your fancy for now. 25-26th Sunshine and showers both come into your life at this time, smile at them both. OPPORTUNITIES: 22-23rd Circumstances conspire to allow you your own way. LIMITING INFLUENCES: 8-10th Many Sagittarians can be far too retreatist for their own good now and need to be more dynamic.

JULY INFLUENCES: 2-3rd Intimate relationships now need some very careful handling. 12-13th Coincidences come your way that will work distinctly in our favour in the days ahead. 29-30th An excellent emphasis is placed upon all social trends and chance encounters. OPPORTUNITIES: 19-20th Self-assurance is not lacking and the typical Sagittarian is clearly on display. LIMITING INFLUENCES: 6-7th You won't get too close to perfection in anything you do at present so be happy for second-best.

AUGUST INFLUENCES: 1-2nd Social matters look good and there is ample chance for travel of all kinds. 18th Things slow down a little and more patience is needed. 22nd Confidence to do whatever takes your fancy is on the increase. 31st End the month with a deifinite effort to shift log-jams. OPPORTUNITIES: 15-17th A time to collect favours and to look at changes professionally. LIMITING INFLUENCES: 3-4th Tie up any loose ends and listen to what is being said around you if you don't want to loose out.

SEPTEMBER INFLUENCES: 2-3rd It's easy to feel that life is getting out of control, so do what you can to slow things down a little. 16-17th Friends and relatives seem to be doing all they can to make you happy at present. 29-30th Communications skills are good and indicate a good time to go for what you want. OPPORTUNITIES: 12-13th Someone, somewhere can do you a particularly good turn if you keep your eyes open. LIMITING INFLUENCES: 26-27th A lull in affairs leads to a blue phase.

OCTOBER INFLUENCES: 4-5th The strongest trends come from the best known people, who you can rely on. 15-16th Working hard at the moment, there may not be too much time to enjoy yourself. 30-31st Emotional support could come from the least expected of directions. OPPORTUNITIES: 9-10th Preparations could be underway for a number of family based celebrations. LIMITING INFLUENCES: 23-24th You are now too inclined to hide your true worth and that means that many opportunities pass you by.

NOVEMBER INFLUENCES: 2-3rd You are quite willing to toe the line in a personal sense and others realise the fact. 10-11th Down in the mouth friends are inclined to turn to you for real support. 24-25th All leisure activities are now well to the fore and offer significant new diversions. OPPORTUNITIES: 5-6th Turn disadvantages in your favour by utilising the great energy you have at present. LIMITING INFLUENCES: 19-21st Not everyone appears to have your best interests at heart for this short period.

DECEMBER INFLUENCES: 1-2nd Right from the start of the month you should be laying down plans for the festive season. 14-15th Mid-month hold-up have more of a bearing on other people than they appear to have on you personally. 25-26th Avoid becoming tired by taking rest in amongst the Christmas celebrations. OPPORTUNITIES: 30-31st The Moon comes to assist you at the end of the year and to help your most important plans along. LIMITING INFLUENCES: 16-17th Slow down the pace of events.

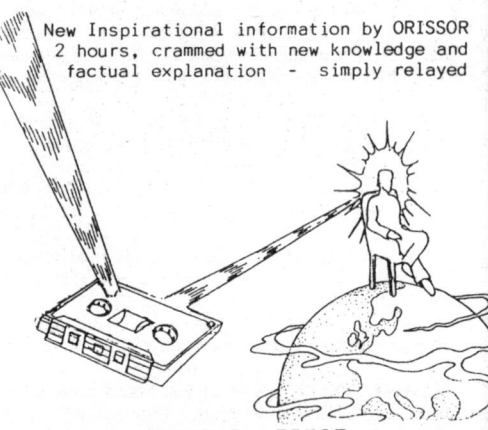

ANNE ROBINSON

When you find four planets in Libra in a horoscope, you know the owner of same will spend a lot of time looking at the broad spectrum of human experience and weighing up different values and ideas, trying to find the perfect balance and the nugget of truth in them all. It is no surprise then to find that Anne Robinson, the presenter of BBC TV's long-running programme "Points of View" and on radio "The Anne Robinson Show," has just this sort of chart: Sun, Neptune, Venus, and Mars in Libra, with a purposeful Moon in Capricorn. Anne was born on September 26th 1944 in Crosby (Liverpool), and although we don't know her time of birth, which would give her Ascendant and the positions of the planets around the birth chart, we can deduce from this strellium in Libra that Anne's driving force is her democratic spirit, her pursuit of justice, and her interest in people. All air signs (Gemini, Libra, Aquarius) live on the mental plane and love to communicate, but Libra is perhaps the most charming and sympathetic of all talkers. This is due to the innate ability to identify with others and to retain an egalitarian spirit whilst in a position of power. This is all the more true because of Anne's Sun being exactly conjunct idealistic Neptune. Hence her attractive style with people and her subtle, strategic manner of presentation. She can exude a real feeling of impartiality in the most awkward of situations, remaining cool and refined all the while she's making a forceful point and getting exactly the reaction she wants. In fact, Venus conjunct Mars means she is actually quite a flirt who loves to stir things up but, of course, in the nicest possible Libran way (who me?? I meant no harm!"). This aspect is the source of Anne's red-headed charisma; it gives her a magnetic manner of expression which catches the public imagination. My serious guess is that this Venus-Mars is quite close to her Ascendant as statistics show that red-heads tend to have a first house Mars. Aspects from maverick Uranus in Gemini add ingenuity and fiery independence: although she centres herself around others' views, she is very much her own person and won't compromise her principles.

The Moon in Capricorn reveals the prudent, ambitious, emotionally-guarded side of Anne's personality. She has tact, a gift for managing people, and a gracious, considerate way of making sure that things will work out the way she wants them to. It would seem that career goals have taken priority over domestic concerns and emotional needs all her life, and that Anne's parental influence directed her out into the world to find success and approval. Her moon in opposition to Saturn in the family sign of Cancer suggests this, as well as the possibility that her ambitious workaholic attitude hides some early sadness and a cynical view of human nature. The Capricorn Moon is also the source of her sardonic wit which is further emphasised by the Moon's trine to a tight Mercury-Jupiter conjunction in Virgo. This is an excellent configuration for the analytical journalist who can handle a myriad of facts and details and, with confident clarity and systematic panache, deliver the obvious pronouncement: the hypocrite revealed. Uranus squares her erudite Mercury-Jupiter which adds just the sort of sting that gives her opinions weight. She enjoys a battle of wits and probably harbours a deep mistrust of authority figures. Her journalistic style is a classic example of the iron hand in the velvet glove: suave, sweet-talking Libra and acerbic Virgo-Capricorn.

It's no surprise that Anne's career made another leap forward when she joined both the TODAY newspaper and the SUNDAY TIMES. The great beneficent Jupiter transits all her Libra planets and trines Uranus throughout '93, bringing luck and opportunity and happy landings. A progressed Sun-Mars conjunction in Scorpio, transited by Jupiter in '94, may bring a very creative period when her will-power and love of enterprise combine to take her towards even more lucrative promotions. Transits in '94 from Uranus and Neptune to her Mars-Venus, however, mean that she must beware of slips and sudden U-turns, especially with regard to personal relationships. Finding a balance, ever the Libran quest, between career goals and emotional needs will occupy her attention at that time.

1994 MAIN UNITED KINGDOM FAIRS AND EVENTS

AGRICULTURAL EVENTS

ABERGAVENNY & Border Counties Show — 'Glebelands', Llanwenarth, Abergavenny: *30th July*
AYR Show — Ayr Racecourse: *4th-5th May*
BAKEWELL Show: *3rd-4th August*
BINGLEY Show — Myrtle Park: *3rd August*
BIRMINGHAM PRIMESTOCK Show — Stafford: *22nd-23rd November(provisional)*
BLACK ISLE SHOW — Muir-of-Ord, Ross-shire: *4th August.*
BORDER UNION Show — Kelso: *29th-30th July*
BROADLANDS Angling and Country Fair: *18th-19th June*
BUCKS County Show — Weedon Park, nr. Aylesbury: *1st September*
CHATSWORTH Country Fair — Bakewell: *3rd-4th September*
CHESHIRE County Show — Tabley, Knutsford: *21st-22nd June*
DENBIGHSHIRE & FLINTSHIRE Agricultural Society Show — Denbigh: *21st August*
DERBYSHIRE County Show — Elvaston Castle, Derby: *date undecided (in May or June)*
DEVON County Show — Westpoint, Clyst St Mary, Exeter: *19th-21st May*
DORCHESTER Agricultural Show — Came Park: *3rd September*
DUMFRIES & LOCKERBIE Show — Park Farm, Dumfries: *6th August*
DURHAM County Agricultural Show — Lambton Park, Chester-le-Street: *16th-17th July*
EAST OF ENGLAND SHOW — Peterborough: *19th-21st July*
EGHAM & THORPE Royal Show — Runnymede: *27th-28th August (provisional)*
ESSEX County Show — Great Leighs, nr Chelmsford: *17th-19th June*
EUROPEAN DAIRY FARMING EVENT — Nat. Agricultural Centre, Stoneleigh, Kenilworth: *22nd-24th September*
GREAT YORKSHIRE Show — Harrogate: *12th-14th July*
HERTS County Show — Redbourn: *28th-29th May*
KENT County Show — Detling, nr. Maidstone: *14th-16th July*
LEICESTERSHIRE County Show — Braunstone Park, Leicester: *2nd May*
LINCOLNSHIRE Show — Grange-de-Lings, Lincoln: *22nd-23rd June*
MID-SOMERSET Show — Shepton Mallet: *21st August*
MONMOUTHSHIRE Show — Monmouth: *25th August*
MONTGOMERYSHIRE Show — Welshpool: *4th June*
NATIONAL SHIRE HORSE Show — Peterborough: *20th March*
NEW FOREST & HAMPSHIRE Show — Brockenhurst: *26th-28th July*
NEWBURY & ROYAL COUNTY OF BERKSHIRE Show — Chievely, Newbury: *17th-18th September*
NORTH SOMERSET Show — Ashton Court, Bristol: *30th May*
NOTTINGHAMSHIRE County Show — Winthorpe, Newark: *6th-7th May*
PEMBROKESHIRE County Show — Withybush, Haverfordwest: *16th-18th August*

ROMSEY Show — Broadlands Park: *10th September*
ROYAL BATH & WEST Show — Shepton Mallet: *1st-4th June*
ROYAL CORNWALL Show — Wadebridge: *9th-11th June*
ROYAL HIGHLAND Show — Ingliston, Edinburgh: *23rd-26th June*
ROYAL LANCASHIRE Show — Chorley: *29th-30th July*
ROYAL NORFOLK Show — New Costessey, Norwich: *29th-30th June*
ROYAL SHOW — National Agricultural Centre, Stoneleigh, Kenilworth: *4th-7th July*
ROYAL SMITHFIELD Show — Earls Court — *27th-30th November.*
ROYAL ULSTER Show & Industrial Exhibition — Balmoral, Belfast: *11th-13th May (provisional)*
ROYAL WELSH Show — Llanelwedd, Builth Wells: *18th-21st July*
ROYAL WELSH AGRICULTURAL WINTER Fair — Llanelwedd, Builth Wells: *6th December*
ST HELENS Show — Sherdley Park: *29th-30th July*
SCOTTISH AGRICULTURAL WINTER Fair: Ingliston, Edinburgh: *23rd-24th November*
SHROPSHIRE & WEST MIDLANDS Show — Shrewsbury: *20th-21st May*
SOUTH OF ENGLAND Show — Ardingley, Haywards Heath: *9th-11th June*
STAFFORDSHIRE County Show — Stafford: *25th-26th May*
SUFFOLK Show — Ipswich: *1st-2nd June*
SURREY County Show — Stoke Park, Guildford: *30th May*
TENDRING HUNDRED Show — Lawford House Park, nr. Manningtree: *9th July*
THAME Show: *15th September*
THREE COUNTIES Show — Malvern: *14th-16th June*
TURRIFF Show: *1st-2nd August*
UNITED COUNTIES Show — Nantyci Showground, Carmarthen: *11th-12th August*
WESTMORLAND County Show — Lane Farm, Crooklands: *8th September*
WOKINGHAM & READING Show — Spencer's Wood, nr. Reading: *4th September*

MISCELLANEOUS

ALDEBURGH Festival of Music and the Arts — Snape Maltings concert hall: *10th-26th June*
BADMINTON Horse Trials: *5th-8th May*
BATH International Festival: *27th May-12th June*
BATTLE OF FLOWERS — Jersey: *11th August*
BBC PROMENADE CONCERTS — Royal Albert Hall, London: *15th July-10th September*
BEVERLEY FOLK Festival: *17th-19th June*
BIGGIN HILL International Air Fair: *18th-19th June*
BRAEMAR Royal Highland Gathering: *3rd September*
BRISTOL TO BOURNEMOUTH Vintage Vehicle Run — from Aston Court: *12th (or possibly 5th) June*
BRITISH INTERNATIONAL MOTOR Show — National Exhibition Centre, Birmingham: *22nd-30th October*
BRITISH ROSE Festival — Hampton Court: *6th-10th July*
CHELSEA Flower Show: *24th-27th May (RHS members only 24th and 25th)*
CHELTENHAM GOLD CUP race meeting: *15th-17th March*

1994 Main United Kingdom Fairs and Events — *continued*

COWES WEEK Regatta — IoW: *30th July-6th August*

CRUFTS Dog Show — National Exhibition Centre, Birmingham: *10th-13th March*

EDINBURGH International Festival: *14th August-3rd September*

EDINBURGH Tattoo — Edinburgh Castle: *5th-27th August*

FA CUP FINAL — Wembley: *7th May (provisional)*

FARNBOROUGH International Aerospace Exhibition and Flying Display, public days: *9th-11th September*

GLYNDEBOURNE Festival Opera — near Lewes: *1st June-25th August*

GOLF — The Open Championship, Ailsa course, Turnberry, Ayrshire: *14th-17th July*

GOODWOOD race meeting: *26th-30th July*

GREAT AUTUMN FLOWER Show — Harrogate: *16th-18th September*

HARROGATE SPRING FLOWER Show: *21st-24th April*

HENLEY Royal Regatta: *29th June-3rd July*

HOPPINGS Fair — Newcastle upon Tyne: *20th-26th June*

HORSE OF THE YEAR Show — Wembley: *5th-9th October*

HULL Fair: *7th-8th, 10th-15th October*

IDEAL HOME PLUS Exhibition — Earls Court: *17th March-10th April*

INTERNATIONAL FESTIVAL OF SCIENCE and Technology — Edinburgh: *7th-23rd April*

KNITTING, NEEDLECRAFT and Design Exhibition — Sandown Park, Esher: *20th-23rd January*

LAWN TENNIS Championships — Wimbledon: *20th June-3rd July*

LLANGOLLEN Int. Musical Eisteddfod: *5th-10th July*

LONDON HARNESS HORSE Parade — Regents Park: *4th April*

LONDON INTERNATIONAL BOAT SHOW — Earls Court: *6th-16th January*

LONDON TO BRIGHTON Veteran Car Run — Hyde Park to Madeira Drive, Brighton: *6th November*

LONDON TO BRIGHTON Historic Commercial Vehicle Run — Crystal Palace to Madeira Drive, Brighton: *1st May*

NOTTINGHAM GOOSE FAIR: *6th-8th October*

NOTTING HILL Carnival — Ladbroke Grove: *28th-29th August*

OLYMPIA INTERNATIONAL SHOWJUMPING Championships: *15th-19th December*

OULD LAMMAS FAIR — Ballycastle: *29th-30th August*

ROYAL ASCOT: *14th-17th June*

ROYAL TOURNAMENT — Earls Court: *19th-30th July*

ROYAL WINDSOR HORSE Show — Home Park, Windsor: *11th-15th May*

SOUTHAMPTON INTERNATIONAL BOAT SHOW — Mayflower Park: *16th-24th September*

SPRING GARDEN Show — Malvern: *6th-8th May*

TOWN & COUNTRY Festival — Nat. Agricultural Centre, Stoneleigh, Kenilworth: *27th-29th August*

Final dates and venues of events listed here, and on the calendar pages, are subject to change. Please check with local organiser/tourist board.

. .63. .

Football Pools Forecast for 1994

The following forecasts of teams likely to draw on the dates given is based on planetary indications and teams' colours. No claim for infallibility is made. Readers should use their own judgement, but forecasts can help in the final selection.

January 1st	Bolton Wanderers, Wolves, Coventry, Leicester.
January 8th	Sheffield Wednesday, Barnsley, Q.P.R., Bristol City.
January 15th	Arsenal, Blackburn Rovers, Fulham, Gillingham.
January 22nd	Derby, Bury, Bradford, Cardiff.
January 29th	Liverpool, Middlesbrough, Mansfield, W.B.A.
February 5th	Blackpool, Huddersfield, Charlton, Newcastle.
February 12th	Manchester United, Bradford, Lincoln City, Wolves.
February 19th	Portsmouth, Brentford, Barnsley, Halifax.
February 26th	Nottingham Forest, Liverpool, Manchester United, Rotherham.
March 5th	Q.P.R., Tottenham, Blackpool, Luton.
March 12th	Charlton, Huddersfield, Chelsea, Fulham.
March 19th	Halifax, Wolves, Gillingham, Manchester City.
March 26th	Burnley, Newcastle, Bristol City, Mansfield.
April 2nd	Millwall, Tottenham, Chelsea, Huddersfield.
April 9th	Fulham, Bury, Mansfield, Cardiff.
April 16th	Bradford, Blackpool, Grimsby, Huddersfield.
April 23rd	Brentford, Derby, Liverpool, Millwall, Chelsea.
April 30th	Gillingham, Everton, Manchester City, Fulham.
May 7th	Halifax, Sheffield Wednesday, Barnsley, Brentford.
May 14th	Manchester United, Mansfield, Wolves, Burnley.
May 21st	Portsmouth, Manchester City, Sunderland, Birmingham.
May 28th	Liverpool, Charlton, Chelsea, Stoke.
September 3rd	Bolton Wanderers, Liverpool, Lincoln, Portsmouth.
September 10th	Sheffield Wednesday, Burnley, Huddersfield. Blackpool.
September 17th	Manchester United, Stoke, Chelsea, Wolves.
September 24th	Tottenham, Everton, Middlesbrough, Burnley.
October 1st	Newcastle, Rotherham, Plymouth, Nottingham Forest.
October 8th	Q.P.R., Bristol City, Halifax, Manchester City.
October 15th	Huddersfield, Chelsea, Birmingham City, Fulham.
October 22nd	Halifax, Leeds, Gillingham, Bradford.
October 29th	Chelsea, Derby, Rotherham, Liverpool.
November 5th	Derby, Wolves, Sheffield Wednesday, Barnsley.
November 12th	Fulham, Chelsea, Millwall, Everton.
November 19th	Portsmouth, Halifax, Q.P.R., Tottenham.
November 26th	Blackburn Rovers, Fulham, Stoke, Chelsea.
December 3rd	Arsenal, Millwall, Luton, Bradford.
December 10th	Bury, Halifax, Cardiff, Brentford.
December 17th	Manchester City, Stoke, Middlesbrough, Portsmouth.
December 24th	Bournemouth, Barnsley, Luton, Q.P.R.

RACING WITH THE FLAT RACE & STEEPLECHASE JOCKEYS IN 1994

ASTROLOGICAL POINTERS TO POSSIBLE WINNING PERIODS

THE ASTROLOGICALLY COMPILED DATES BELOW ARE PRESENTED TO RACEGOERS IN THE HOPE THAT THEY WILL POINT THE WAY TO SOME SUCCESSFUL WINNING PERIODS DURING THE 1994 RACING SEASON.

Pat EDDERY, born 18th March, 1952, should be noted on 2 y.o.'s, 3 y.o.'s and short priced older horses. His favourable periods are: March 16th, 17th, 21st to 30th, April 1st to 4th, 6th to 23rd (9th to 11th, 13th to 16th specially recommended), 26th, 27th, May 1st to 16th (10th to 13th s.r.), 20th to 31st (21st, 23rd to 25th s.r.), June 2nd to 16th (4th, 14th s.r.), 22nd to 25th (24th s.r.), 28th, 29th (29th s.r.), July 4th to 12th (5th, 8th, 11th s.r.), 16th to 27th (19th, 22nd, 23rd, 25th s.r.), August 1st to 4th, 8th to 12th (8th s.r.), 16th to 19th (16th to 18th s.r.), 23rd to 31st (31st s.r.), September 1st to 30th (4th to 10th, 23rd to 30th s.r.), October 1st to 7th (1st, 5th s.r.), 20th to 28th, 31st, November 1st to 4th, 17th to 19th.

A. MUNRO, born 14th January, 1967, should be noted on 3 y.o.'s. His favourable periods are: March 16th to 23rd, 25th, 26th, 29th to 31st, April 1st, 4th, 5th, 7th to 9th (8th s.r.), May 1st to 3rd (1st, 2nd s.r.), 6th to 9th (6th s.r.), 13th to 23rd (16th to 23rd s.r.), 26th to 28th, 31st, June 1st to 3rd (1st s.r.), 6th to 24th (8th to 11th, 21st to 24th s.r.), 27th, 30th, July 1st to 12th (2nd to 4th, 9th to 11th s.r.), 18th to 25th (21st to 23rd s.r.), 30th, August 2nd to 6th (5th, 6th s.r.), 9th, 13th to 18th (15th, 17th s.r.), 24th to 30th (25th, 27th to 30th s.r.), September 3rd, 5th to 9th (8th s.r.,) 13th, 16th to 22nd, 26th to 28th, 30th, October 1st to 5th, 8th to 10th, 17th to 20th, 24th to 31st (24th to 27th s.r.), November 1st to 4th, 7th to 11th (9th, 10th s.r.), 16th to 19th (19th s.r.).

T. QUINN, born 2nd December, 1961, should be noted on 2 y.o.'s and 3 y.o.'s. He will have a very successful season. His favourable periods are: March 19th to 31st (19th, 26th, 28th to 31st s.r.), April 4th to 9th (8th, 9th s.r.), 12th to 16th (12th to 15th s.r.), 18th to 30th (22nd, 25th, 30th s.r.), May 1st to 20th (2nd to 4th, 7th, 16th, 19th s.r.), 24th to 27th, 31st, June 1st to 30th (1st, 4th, 6th, 10th, 11th, 13th to 16th, 20th, 23rd to 27th s.r.), July 1st to 13th (1st, 2nd, 5th, 7th, 9th s.r.), 19th to 31st (22nd, 23rd, 25th s.r.), August 1st to 31st (1st to 3rd, 21st to 24th, 27th to 31st s.r.), September 1st to 27th (2nd, 5th, 6th, 19th to 21st, 26th, 27th s.r.), 30th, October 1st to 31st (1st, 3rd, 21st to 24th, 27th to 31st s.r.), November 1st, 5th, 16th to 18th.

M. ROBERTS, born 17th May, 1954, should be noted on 3 y.o.'s and 4 y.o.'s. His favourable periods are: March 21st, 22nd, 28th, 29th, April 4th, 8th, 9th, 18th to 29th (22nd, 23rd s.r.), May 4th to 7th, 10th, 16th to 18th (17th s.r.), 23rd to 27th, June 4th to 7th, 11th, 15th to 17th (16th, 17th s.r.), 21st to 30th (24th, 27th to 29th s.r.), July 1st to 9th (5th to 7th s.r.), 13th, 14th, 18th, 19th, 25th to 29th, August 2nd, 8th to 11th (8th to 10th s.r.), 18th to 25th (18th s.r.), 31st, September 1st to 3rd (1st to 3rd s.r.), 9th, 10th, 19th to 24th (20th to 22nd s.r.), October 3rd to 28th (7th to 25th s.r.), November 2nd to 8th (5th to 7th s.r.), 18th, 19th.

R. DUNWOODY, born 18th January, 1964, should be noted on 3 y.o.'s and older horses. He will have an outstandingly good year. His favourable periods are: January 1st to 31st (1st to 10th, 15th to 17th, 21st to 25th, 31st s.r.), February 7th to 19th (10th to 12th, 14th to 16th s.r.), 28th, March 1st to 10th (1st to 4th s.r.), 15th to 19th, 21st to 23rd, 31st, April 1st to 30th (8th, 9th, 15th to 18th, 20th to 30th s.r.), May 2nd to 31st (2nd, 3rd, 16th to 21st, 28th to 31st s.r.), August 1st to 31st (1st to 3rd s.r.), Spetember 1st to 22nd (1st to 5th, 19th to 21st s.r.), 26th to 30th, October 3rd to 6th, 18th to 21st, 24th to 31st (24th to 29th s.r.), November 1st to 8th (5th to 30th s.r.), December 1st to 5th (2nd, 5th, 17th, 19th s.r.).

G. McCOURT, born 17th August, 1959, should be noted on 3 y.o.'s, 4 y.o.'s and older horses. He will have a very good year. His favourable periods are: January 1st to 31st (1st to 24th s.r.), February 1st to 12th (9th to 12th s.r.), 14th to 19th (16th to 18th s.r.), March 1st to 22nd (3rd to 18th s.r.), 28th, 30th, 31st, April 1st to 30th (10th to 23rd s.r.), May 2nd to 7th (6th s.r.), 12th to 25th (16th to 19th, 21st s.r.), 31st, August 1st to 31st (8th to 13th, 16th to 18th, 23rd to 31st s.r.), September 1st to 28th (1st to 23rd, 26th to 28th s.r.), 29th, 30th, October 1st to 7th (4th s.r.), 16th to 31st (21st to 29th s.r.), November 1st to 30th (1st to 5th, 14th to 30th s.r.), December 1st to 31st (1st to 19th, 21st to 29th s.r.).

ADRIAN McGUIRE, born 29th April, 1971, should be noted on chiefly on 3 y.o.'s and 4 y.o.'s but he may also win on 5 y.o.'s. His favourable periods are: January 1st to 31st (1st, 11th to 13th, 22nd to 24th, 29th to 31st s.r.), February 1st to 14th, 17th to 19th s.r.), March 1st to 31st (2nd to 4th, 8th to 10th, 18th, 28th, 29th s.r.), April 1st to 30th (9th to 11th, 15th, 16th, 26th, 27th s.r.), May 1st to 31st (5th to 7th, 18th to 20th, 24th to 26th s.r.), August 10th to 12th, 18th to 31st (20th to 31st s.r.), September 1st, 10th to 13th, 27th to 30th, October 4th to 31st (4th to 13th s.r.), November 1st, 2nd, 9th to 30th (19th to 30th s.r.), December 1st to 31st (1st to 3rd, 13th to 31st s.r.).

P. NIVEN, born 7th August, 1964, should be noted on 3 y.o.'s, 4 y.o.'s and 5 y.o.'s. He will win many races. His favourable periods are: January 1st to 13th (6th to 8th s.r.), 22nd to 31st (22nd to 29th s.r.), February 3rd to 19th (2nd, 3rd, 10th to 18th s.r.), 24th to 28th, March 1st to 9th (4th, 5th, 7th s.r.), 16th to 21st, 24th to 26th, 31st, April 1st to 6th, 13th to 26th (16th to 21st s.r.), May 2nd to 5th, 9th to 24th (17th to 19th s.r.), 26th to 31st (30th, 31st s.r.), August 1st to 30th (1st to 5th, 9th to 20th s.r.), September 1st to 30th (3rd, 6th, 7th, 19th to 30th s.r.), October 1st to 4th (1st to 4th s.r.), 20th to 31st (20th to 31st s.r.), November 1st to 30th (10th to 21st, 26th to 30th s.r.), December 1st to 31st (1st to 13th, 19th to 22nd s.r.).

. .68. .

RACING WITH THE FLAT RACE & STEEPLECHASE TRAINERS IN 1994

ASTROLOGICAL POINTERS TO POSSIBLE WINNING PERIODS

THE ASTROLOGICALLY COMPILED DATES BELOW ARE PRESENTED TO RACEGOERS IN THE HOPE THAT THEY WILL POINT THE WAY TO SOME SUCCESSFUL WINNING PERIODS DURING THE 1994 RACING SEASON.

The favourable periods of National Hunt Trainers

D NICHOLSON, born 19th March, 1939, should have the following winning periods: January 1st, 11th to 13th (12th, 13th specially recommended), 20th to 27th, February 10th, 11th, 22nd to 28th (25th, 26th s.r.), March 1st to 5th (1st, 2nd s.r.), 11th to 31st (22nd to 28th s.r.), April 5th to 12th (11th, 12th s.r.), 18th, 19th, 26th to 28th. May 1st, 2nd, 11th to 14th (11th, 12th s.r.), 26th to 28th, August 13th to 15th, 19th to 24th, 29th, 30th (29th, 30th s.r.), September 1st to 9th, 14th to 30th (29th, 30th s.r.), October 1st to 31st (8th to 15th, 29th to 31st s.r.), November 1st to 30th (8th to 11th, 14th, 15th s.r.), December 1st to 6th (6th to 10th, 13th, 14th, 27th to 30th s.r.).

M. PIPE, born 29th May, 1945, should have the following winning periods: January 1st to 17th (3rd to 5th, 15th to 17th s.r.), 21st, 22nd, 24th to 31st (27th, 28th, 31st s.r.), February 1st to 15th (8th to 12th s.r.), 21st, 28th, March 1st to 5th, 16th to 22nd, 28th, 29th, April 8th to 11th, 16th to 23rd (22nd, 23rd s.r.), 27th to 30th, May 4th, 5th, 16th to 19th (16th to 18th s.r.), 30th, August 2nd to 4th, 8th to 11th, 17th, 18th, 29th to 31st, October 13th to 31st (22nd to 26th s.r.), November 1st to 9th (2nd to 6th s.r.), 14th to 30th (25th s.r.), December 1st, 14th to 17th, 31st.

Mrs G. R. REVELEY, born 22nd November, 1940, should be noted for her 4 y.o. and 5 y.o. horses. Her favourable periods are: January 1st to 14th (1st to 11th s.r.), 20th to 22nd, February 1st to 28th (9th to 15th s.r.), March 1st to 12th, 18th, 19th, 21st, April 19th to 9th (6th to 9th s.r.), 18th to 30th (25th to 29th s.r.), May 1st to 13th, 16th to 19th, 25th to 31st s.r.), August 1st to 31st (8th to 12th, 30th, 31st s.r.), September 1st to 13th (1st to 10th s.r.), 23rd to 28th, October 19th to 27th, November 1st to 5th, 8th to 30th (21st to 24th s.r.), December 10th to 31st.

The favourable periods of Flat Racing Trainers

J. BERRY, born 7th October, 1937, should be noted when he runs short priced 2 and 3 y.o.'s. His favourable periods are: March 16th, 17th, 21st (s.r.), 22nd, 28th to 30th (29th s.r.), April 2nd, 8th, 9th, 11th to 29th (14th to 16th, 22nd, 23rd, 26th to 29th s.r.), May 4th to 6th, 9th, 10th, 17th to 19th (17th to 19th s.r.), 21st, 24th to 26th, 30th, June 3rd, 4th, 6th to 8th, 11th, 15th to 30th (16th, 17th, 27th to 29th s.r.), July 1st to 4th, 7th, 8th, 11th, 12th, 18th to 21st (20th s.r.), 25th to 28th (26th, 27th s.r.), August 3rd to 13th (8th to 11th s.r.), 17th to 19th (17th, 18th s.r.), 23rd, 24th, September 1st to 3rd, 8th to 19th, 21st to 28th, October 1st to 31st (3rd to 11th, 24th to 26th s.r.), November 1st to 15th (1st to 5th s.r.).

P. F. I. COLE, born on 11th September, 1941, should win many races with his 2 and 3 y.o.'s. His favourable periods are: March 15th to 19th (15th to 18th s.r.), 21st, 22nd, 26th to 31st, April 1st, 2nd, 8th to 12th (9th, 11th s.r.), 15th, 16th, 22nd, 23rd, 27th to 29th, May 1st to 6th (1st to 3rd s.r.), 16th to 20th (16th to 18th s.r.), 30th, 31st, June 7th to 18th (11th, 16th to 18th s.r.), 24th, 25th, July 1st to 8th (2nd to 8th s.r.), 18th to 21st (18th to 20th s.r.), August 1st to 5th (2nd to 4th s.r.), 9th to 20th (18th, 19th s.r.), September 1st to 18th (1st to 3rd, 7th to 15th sr.), 21st to 29th, October 3rd to 5th, 18th, 19th, 24th to 27th, 31st, November 1st to 6th (1st to 4th s.r.), 17th to 19th.

R. HANNON, born 30th May, 1945, should win many races with his 2 y.o.'s and 3 y.o.'s. His fortunate periods are: March 17th to 23rd, 29th to 31st, April 9th, 11th to 25th (11th, 22nd, 23rd s.r.), 28th to 30th, May 5th, 6th, 17th to 19th, 30th, 31st, June 8th to 13th, 22nd to 30th (24th, 27th to 30th s.r.), July 1st to 8th (7th s.r.), 19th to 22nd (21st s.r.), August 3rd, 4th, 9th to 12th, 18th, 19th, September 2nd to 29th (3rd, 16th s.r.), October 12th to 31st (24th to 28th, 31st s.r.), November 1st, 2nd, 19th to 26th.

M. STOUTE, born 22nd October, 1945, should do well with his 2 y.o.'s, 3 y.o.'s. Older mares should also do well. His fortunate periods are: March 22nd to 25th, 29th to 31st, April 1st, 2nd, 4th to 6th, 11th to 13th, 16th to 30th (16th to 20th, 28th to 30th s.r.), May 7th to 12th (10th to 12th s.r.), June 22nd to 31st (30th, 31st s.r.), July 1st to 6th (6th, 7th, 16th to 21st, 27th to 30th s.r.), July 1st to 31st (1st to 15th, 27th to 30th s.r.), August 1st to 6th, 10th to 13th, 20th to 29th (25th to 27th s.r.), September 12th to 19th (13th to 15th s.r.), October 1st to 24th (7th to 20th s.r.), November 1st to 21st (10th to 15th s.r.).

Greyhound Racing Numbers Forecasts
This Trap Numbers Forecast may Point the Way to Possible Success in 1994

In the following forecasts, based on a combination of the numbers ruling the area and of the most prominent fortunate planetary number during the period given, the system is followed of giving each area of the country the most propitious dates for that area and the lucky numbers operative between those dates. The first number should be the winner and the second number should be the second dog, and these numbers are printed in bold type below.

While making no claim to infallibility, the compiler of this feature hopes that the information set out below will prove helpful and beneficial to those readers who enjoy an occasional jaunt to the Greyhound Racing Meetings in the particular area mentioned.

LONDON

Jan.	4/15	**6 3**	Feb.	1/10	**2 1**	Mar.	4/11	**4 2**
	18/27	**3 1**		15/24	**2 3**		19/30	**6 5**
Apr.	5/14	**4 3**	May	3/15	**6 1**	June	1/11	**3 4**
	19/29	**2 4**		16/25	**3 1**		16/27	**5 6**
July	3/12	**2 1**	Aug.	2/11	**6 2**	Sep.	8/16	**4 3**
	15/27	**2 4**		15/26	**3 4**		17/26	**3 4**
Oct.	4/15	**6 2**	Nov.	4/12	**1 6**	Dec.	1/11	**6 5**
	19/31	**5 2**		16/28	**4 1**		19/30	**2 4**

BIRMINGHAM

Jan.	1/13	**3 1**	Feb.	4/11	**2 6**	Mar.	2/10	**3 5**
	17/25	**2 5**		19/28	**5 4**		17/24	**5 6**
Apr.	4/14	**6 4**	May	1/10	**1 3**	June	3/13	**4 6**
	22/30	**6 4**		17/27	**5 3**		22/29	**3 6**
July	4/13	**5 2**	Aug.	3/11	**2 5**	Sep.	1/9	**4 3**
	20/30	**6 4**		18/29	**3 2**		16/27	**1 3**
Oct.	1/12	**4 6**	Nov.	7/17	**2 5**	Dec.	5/14	**5 1**
	19/28	**3 6**		19/28	**1 4**		16/25	**4 1**

MANCHESTER

Jan.	1/11	**2 6**	Feb.	3/13	**6 1**	Mar.	4/15	**5 6**
	18/30	**2 3**		15/25	**1 2**		18/28	**2 3**
Apr.	1/10	**4 3**	May	2/12	**6 4**	June	1/9	**3 2**
	16/29	**2 6**		18/27	**1 2**		15/27	**6 2**
July	1/12	**3 4**	Aug.	4/13	**1 2**	Sep.	2/10	**1 6**
	19/27	**5 1**		16/26	**5 1**		16/27	**6 3**
Oct.	6/15	**1 6**	Nov.	4/15	**3 2**	Dec.	7/16	**3 1**
	17/28	**6 5**		18/27	**5 4**		19/29	**5 4**

NEWCASTLE

Jan.	5/16	**1 6**	Feb.	3/12	**3 5**	Mar.	2/11	**5 1**
	18/27	**4 2**		16/27	**6 5**		16/26	**2 6**
Apr.	1/12	**1 4**	May	5/14	**3 2**	June	4/12	**4 5**
	19/28	**5 2**		17/28	**2 1**		16/27	**1 6**
July	1/10	**5 6**	Aug.	5/13	**4 5**	Sep.	1/9	**4 3**
	20/31	**1 4**		19/28	**2 5**		18/28	**5 2**
Oct.	1/13	**4 1**	Nov.	1/11	**3 5**	Dec.	7/15	**6 3**
	18/29	**1 5**		17/26	**1 4**		18/29	**1 5**

SHEFFIELD

Jan.	1/12	**3 6**	Feb.	4/14	**3 4**	Mar.	1/13	**1 4**
	20/30	**4 5**		16/26	**3 5**		20/30	**2 5**
Apr.	2/14	**2 3**	May	5/16	**4 1**	June	6/17	**2 3**
	17/26	**4 3**		21/31	**4 5**		22/30	**5 1**
July	2/14	**4 1**	Aug.	5/15	**6 3**	Sep.	2/11	**5 3**
	19/30	**4 6**		20/29	**5 3**		13/26	**3 2**
Oct.	2/11	**2 4**	Nov.	4/14	**4 6**	Dec.	6/13	**3 5**
	19/29	**4 2**		19/28	**6 1**		19/28	**2 1**

WALES

Jan.	1/12	**6 4**	Feb.	4/15	**5 2**	Mar.	1/10	**4 2**
	17/26	**4 6**		22/31	**5 3**		15/27	**5 3**
Apr.	5/14	**3 6**	May	3/11	**4 5**	June	8/16	**6 2**
	19/28	**1 3**		20/31	**5 2**		19/27	**1 5**
July	5/13	**2 4**	Aug.	6/15	**3 4**	Sep.	3/15	**6 1**
	21/30	**3 1**		20/30	**1 5**		19/28	**3 1**
Oct.	6/17	**3 6**	Nov.	1/12	**5 3**	Dec.	2/13	**1 3**
	20/29	**5 4**		19/27	**2 1**		15/27	**2 5**

SOUTH OF ENGLAND

Jan.	5/13	**2 4**	Feb.	4/13	**1 2**	Mar.	1/12	**4 6**
	18/27	**1 3**		20/30	**6 2**		18/29	**1 5**
Apr.	4/14	**6 5**	May	4/16	**3 6**	June	2/13	**1 4**
	19/29	**4 3**		18/26	**2 6**		16/27	**6 1**
July	8/19	**5 1**	Aug.	1/11	**1 2**	Sep.	4/12	**2 3**
	23/29	**5 2**		16/28	**3 5**		16/29	**4 1**
Oct.	1/10	**4 5**	Nov.	4/14	**6 3**	Dec.	8/17	**5 6**
	17/28	**1 3**		17/28	**2 1**		20/29	**2 4**

BINGO
YOUR LUCKY DATES IN 1994

CAPRICORN (BIRTHDAYS DECEMBER 22nd to JANUARY 20th) — January 1st to March 9th, April 2nd to June 14th, July 12th to September 3rd, September 28th to December 31st.

AQUARIUS (BIRTHDAYS JANUARY 21st to FEBRUARY 19th) — January 28th to April 1st, April 27th to July 10th, August 8th to September 6th, October 20th to December 18th.

PISCES (BIRTHDAYS FEBRUARY 20th to MARCH 20th) — February 1st to April 26th, May 22nd to August 7th, November 11th to December 31st.

ARIES (BIRTHDAYS MARCH 21st to APRIL 20th) — January 14th to February 12th, March 9th to May 20th, June 18th to September 7th, October 21st to December 30th.

TAURUS (BIRTHDAYS APRIL 21st to MAY 21st) — January 1st to February 12th, April 2nd to June 15th, July 12th to September 8th, December 20th to 31st.

GEMINI (BIRTHDAYS MAY 22nd to JUNE 21st) — January 14th to March 19th, April 9th to May 28th, August 3rd to September 27th, October 20th to December 19th.

CANCER (BIRTHDAYS JUNE 22nd to JULY 22nd) — January 1st to April 9th, May 22nd to August 17th, September 28th to December 18th.

LEO (BIRTHDAYS JULY 23rd to AUGUST 23rd) — January 28th to March 7th, April 15th to August 16th, October 4th to December 12th.

VIRGO (BIRTHDAYS AUGUST 24th to SEPTEMBER 23rd) — January 1st to February 21st, March 19th to May 9th, July 10th to September 3rd, November 11th to December 31st.

LIBRA (BIRTHDAYS SEPTEMBER 24th to OCTOBER 23rd) — February 13th to April 9th, May 21st to July 9th, August 8th to September 6th, October 20th to December 25th.

SCORPIO (BIRTHDAYS OCTOBER 24th to NOVEMBER 22nd) — January 28th to March 31st, May 24th to July 3rd, September 8th to December 31st.

SAGITTARIUS (BIRTHDAYS NOVEMBER 23rd to DECEMBER 21st) — January 19th to April 1st, June 15th to July 11th, August 8th to September 7th, October 5th to December 11th.

BEST SOWING AND PLANTING TIMES
FOR THE GARDEN IN THE YEAR 1994

WHEN TO PLANT OR SOW TO GET THE BEST RESULTS BY THE MOON

PEAS, BEANS, FLOWERING VEGETABLES AND PLANTS WHICH PRODUCE FRUIT ABOVE THE GROUND SHOULD ALWAYS BE SOWN WHEN THE MOON IS GOING TO THE FULL. POTATOES AND ROOT CROPS SHOULD ALWAYS BE SOWN WHEN THE MOON IS LOW AND BELOW THE EARTH. IF YOU SOW, PLANT OR RE-POT AT THE TIMES SET OUT BELOW IT IS REASONABLY CERTAIN YOU WILL HAVE REALLY FINE RESULTS.

The following dates are the most propitious for sowing and planting in 1994

JANUARY   10, 11 ..... 9.00 to 10.45 a.m. ..... 12.30 to 3.05 p.m.
     26, 27 ..... 9.10 to 10.35 a.m. ..... 12.50 to 3.50 p.m.

FEBRUARY   9, 10 ..... 8.40 to 10.50 a.m. ..... 1.20 to 4.30 p.m.
     28 ..... 8.25 to 10.15 a.m. ..... 11.50 to 2.50 p.m. ..... 3.30 to 4.50 p.m.
Continue to sow peas, beans, onions, spinach, savoys, lettuce, celery, cauliflowers, carrots, parsnips and radishes. Cut early kidney potatoes for seed and put them in a stove or hotbed in order to start them for planting out.

MARCH   1 ..... 8.05 to 10.10 a.m. ..... 12.30 to 3.15 p.m. ..... 4.50 to 5.10 p.m.
     12, 13 ..... 7.45 to 9.50 a.m. ..... 11.40 to 2.30 p.m. ..... 4.20 to 5.25 p.m.
     27, 28 ..... 7.40 to 10.05 a.m. ..... 11.25 to 2.10 p.m. ..... 3.55 to 5.35 p.m.
Vegetables should be put into the ground this month. Sow asparagus, celery, cauliflower, spinach, onions, carrots, peas, beans, savoy, parsnips, radishes, etc. Plant red cabbage and sea-kale.

APRIL   11, 12 ..... 7.20 to 9.35 a.m. ..... 11.40 to 2.20 p.m. ..... 4.00 to 6.10 p.m.
     24, 25 ..... 7.35 to 9.50 a.m. ..... 12.10 to 2.45 p.m. ..... 4.25 to 6.20 p.m.
Plant rhubarb, artichokes, asparagus, sea-kale, Dutch-turnips, German greens and small salading. Earth up peas, tie up lettuce, and in dry weather water seed in bed.

MAY   9, 10 ..... 7.50 to 10.25 a.m. ..... 12.40 to 2.50 p.m. ..... 5.10 to 6.40 p.m.
     24, 25 ..... 7.15 to 9.40 a.m. ..... 11.25 to 2.10 p.m. ..... 4.30 to 5.50 pm.
Sow peas, cucumber, red beet for pickling, and a full crop of kidney beans. Transplant cabbage, winter greens, cauliflower and celery. Hoe and stake peas, water newly-planted crops.

JUNE   9, 10 ..... 7.30 to 10.20 a.m. ..... 12.40 to 3.20 p.m. ..... 6.10 to 8.25 p.m.
     23, 24 ..... 7.15 to 10.30 a.m. ..... 1.10 to 4.20 p.m. ..... 6.40 to 8.45 p.m.
Top beans and peas to assist the filling of the pods. Set kidney beans and transplant cabbage, savoy, broccoli and sow turnips. Thin out onions, leeks, parsnips and early turnips.

JULY   7, 8 ..... 7.10 to 9.20 a.m. ..... 12.40 to 3.05 p.m. ..... 5.25 to 7.50 p.m.
     21, 22 ..... 7.35 to 10.10 a.m. ..... 1.25 to 3.20 p.m. ..... 6.30 to 9.00 p.m.
Sow turnips, radishes, etc. Plant out broccoli cauliflowers, savoys, leeks and winter cabbages and earth up celery. Lift full-grown winter onions.

AUGUST   7, 8 ..... 7.20 to 9.45 a.m. ..... 12.50 to 2.45 p.m. ..... 5.15 to 8.35 p.m.
     21, 22 ..... 7.10 to 10.10 a.m. ..... 1.20 to 3.50 p.m. ..... 7.10 to 9.15 p.m.
Sow early cabbages and parsley for the succeeding year, also spinach, broccoli and cauliflower to stand the winter, transplant broccoli, savoys, and cauliflowers.

SEPTEMBER   4, 5 ..... 7.25 to 10.25 a.m. ..... 1.35 to 3.30 p.m. ..... 6.50 to 8.50 p.m.
     18, 19 ..... 7.40 to 10.05 a.m. ..... 12.45 to 3.10 p.m. ..... 5.50 to 7.20 p.m.
Plant savoys, broccoli, cauliflowers, leeks, celery, pull onions if tips appear drying. Prick out cabbage.

OCTOBER   5, 6 ..... 8.15 to 10.35 a.m. ..... 12.05 to 2.55 p.m. ..... 4.35 to 6.20 p.m.
     18, 19 ..... 8.40 to 10.20 a.m. ..... 11.50 to 2.10 p.m. ..... 3.20 to 4.50 p.m.
Plant some radishes, early cabbages, cauliflowers, mint and tarragon in frames for winter use.

NOVEMBER   2, 3 ..... 9.00 to 10.40 a.m. ..... 12.05 to 2.20 p.m. ..... 3.35 to 5.00 p.m.
     18, 19 ..... 9.15 to 11.10 a.m. ..... 1.30 to 4.10 p.m.
Dig in ground where the crops are carried off and which is not intended to plant again till spring. Shallots are readily propagated by offsets.

DECEMBER   1, 2 ..... 9.10 to 11.20 a.m. ..... 12.50 to 3.35 p.m.
     18, 19 ..... 9.15 to 11.30 a.m. ..... 1.25 to 3.50 p.m.
Earth up celery. Sow small salad in warm borders, covered with mats.

The above times are Greenwich Mean Time. Allowances must be made for British Summer Time.

. .76. .

Angler's Guide for 1994
WHEN TO FISH AND THE BEST TIMES
THE TIME CHART THAT BRINGS GOOD RESULTS

JANUARY — Salmon season opens but high water can be a problem. Cold water makes other freshwater fish lethargic. Larger rivers are best bet, with stillwaters generally unproductive except for pike, which will probably feed best on deadbaits. The change of big roach on bread, ledgering best method. Chub will feed on most days, and bream in coloured water. Cod and whiting will provide best sea sport, with flounders in harbours. Best days 6th, 7th, 15th, 16th, 17th (A.M.), 25th, 26th.

FEBRUARY — Snow and frosts make chance of big catches of freshwater fish unlikely, but specimen pike, roach and zander are a possibility. Use smaller baits and smaller hooks for best results. Salmon anglers should be ready for big springers. Cod starting to get more scarce, but fish will be bigger. Still plenty of whiting and some spurdog from boats. Best days 2nd (P.M.), 3rd, 4th (A.M.), 11th (P.M.), 12th, 13th (A.M.), 21st (P.M.), 22nd, 23rd (A.M.).

MARCH — Sport patchy, but mild days can provide some spectacular catches in freshwater. All species can be caught, even tench and carp. Freshwater season ends in most areas on March 14, with many trout waters opening on following day. Most trout will be caught in deeper water. Cod and whiting leaving in most areas, but spurdog showing well from boats. Best days 1st (P.M.), 2nd, 3rd (P.M.), 10th (P.M.), 11th, 12th, 20th (P.M.), 21st, 22nd.

APRIL — Most trout waters open on 1st. Stillwater trouting will be easy with most flies taking fish, but river fish will be more wary. Black bream showing for some boat anglers, but otherwise sport will be mainly with flatfish and dogfish. Wreck anglers can get good hauls of ling and conger. Some good rays from shallower water. Best days 7th, 8th, 9th, (A.M.), 17th, 18th, 19th (A.M.), 25th (P.M.), 26th, 27th (A.M.).

MAY — Warmer weather will start to bring trout up in the water and floating lines will start to pay off on stillwaters. Some bass showing for beach anglers, with crab as best bait, accounting for flatfish and eels too. Good time for plaice on ragworm from harbours. Best days 4th 5th, 6th (A.M), 14th, 15th, 16th (A.M.), 23rd, 24th, 31st (P.M.)

JUNE — Freshwater season opens in most areas on the 16th. Very big carp, tench and bream from stillwaters, along with big catches of chub in streamier parts of rivers. All baits will take fish, though sport may be patchy on first few days. Bass now starting to show in most areas, and mullet moving into harbours. Mackerel starting to show, and first shark will be caught. Crab and worm will take most shore fish, with fish baits productive on boats. Best days 1st, 2nd, 10th (P.M.), 11th, 12th (A.M.), 19th, 20th, 21st (A.M.), 28th, 29th, 30th (A.M.).

JULY — The best month for freshwater fishing on both rivers and stillwaters. All baits will catch fish. Sweetcorn and other particle baits like to prove successful for big tench and carp. Fish will be in the flow on most running water. Good catches of most species will be taken, particularly barbel and bream. Evenings will usually be best time for trout fishing. Sea trout arriving on many rivers. Summer sea fish well in, and mackerel will attract tope and shark. Plenty of bass, and mullet starting to feed in harbours and around piers. Best days 7th (P.M.), 8th, 9th, 16th (P.M.), 17th, 18th (A.M.), 25th, 26th, 27th (A.M.).

AUGUST — Low water can be a problem in many areas. On running waters, fish areas where there is most flow. Night or late evening fishing may be best after hot days on stillwater. Big barbel catches will be made. Sea fishing at its best with all summer species being caught on most baits. Chance of very big hauls of pollack, ling and conger from wrecks. Best days 4th, 5th, 6th (A.M.), 12th (P.M.), 13th, 14th, 21st (P.M.), 22nd, 23rd, 31st.

SEPTEMBER — Chance of big barbel, and very big roach and dace hauls on maggot or caster. Stillwaters starting to tail off, but good bream, tench and carp can still be landed. Good time for eels on rivers. Summer sea fish starting to move off, but some good bass still around on sandeel and crab. Early whiting will be caught. Trout fishing now getting harder. Best days 1st, 2nd (A.M.), 9th, 10th, 11th (A.M.), 17th (P.M.), 18th, 19th, 27th (P.M.), 28th, 29th.

OCTOBER — Rivers now offer best sport, with stillwaters generally unproductive. Possibility of good roach, dace and chub catches with caster or maggot as best bait. Float fishing generally best. Chance of big catches of salmon with extra water. Beaches now producing whiting and occasional cod. Best days 6th (P.M.), 7th, 8th (A.M.), 15th, 16th, 17th (A.M.), 25th, 26th, 27th (A.M.).

November — Rain and colder water will make fishing harder in all areas, though fish will shoal tighter and good chub or bream catches can be taken. Feed more lightly for best results and scale down hook and line sizes. Some good pike can be taken. Cod now well in, with lugworm as best bait in most areas. Best days 2nd (P.M.), 3rd, 4th, 11th (P.M.), 12th, 13th (A.M.), 21st (P.M.), 22nd, 23rd (A.M.), 26th, 27th, 28th (A.M.), 30th (P.M.)

DECEMBER — Although the weather can make fishing uncomfortable, this can still be a good month, though it may be necessary to move around for fish. It will generally be a case of taking a couple from each swim. Chub are a good bet except in coloured water, when bread will take bream. Roach will be less prolific but bigger. The days after storms can bring catches from beaches, where night fishing will generally bring best results. Cod and whiting will be main quarry. Best days 1st, 2nd (A.M.), 8th (P.M.), 9th, 10th, 18th (P.M.), 19th, 20th, 27th (P.M.), 28th, 29th (A.M.).

Lighting-up Times for 1994

Day	Jan. h.m.	Feb. h.m.	Mar. h.m.	Apr. h.m.	May h.m.	June h.m.	July h.m.	Aug. h.m.	Sep. h.m.	Oct. h.m.	Nov. h.m.	Dec. h.m.
1	16.32	17.19	18.10	20.03	20.53	21.38	21.51	21.18	20.17	19.08	17.04	16.25
2	16.33	17.21	18.11	20.04	20.54	21.39	21.50	21.17	20.14	19.06	17.02	16.25
3	16.34	17.23	18.13	20.06	20.56	21.40	21.50	21.15	20.12	19.04	17.00	16.24
4	16.35	17.25	18.15	20.08	20.58	21.41	21.49	21.13	20.10	19.01	16.58	16.23
5	16.37	17.26	18.17	20.09	20.59	21.42	21.49	21.12	20.08	18.59	16.57	16.23
6	16.38	17.28	18.18	20.11	21.01	21.43	21.48	21.10	20.05	18.57	16.55	16.23
7	16.39	17.30	18.20	20.13	21.02	21.43	21.48	21.08	20.03	18.55	16.53	16.22
8	16.40	17.32	18.22	20.14	21.04	21.44	21.47	21.06	20.01	18.52	16.52	16.22
9	16.42	17.34	18.24	20.16	21.06	21.45	21.46	21.04	19.59	18.50	16.50	16.22
10	16.43	17.36	18.25	20.18	21.07	21.46	21.46	21.02	19.56	18.48	16.49	16.22
11	16.44	17.37	18.27	20.19	21.09	21.47	21.45	21.01	19.54	18.46	16.47	16.22
12	16.46	17.39	18.29	20.21	21.10	21.47	21.44	20.59	19.52	18.44	16.46	16.21
13	16.47	17.41	18.30	20.23	21.12	21.48	21.43	20.57	19.49	18.42	16.44	16.21
14	16.49	17.43	18.32	20.24	21.13	21.48	21.42	20.55	19.47	18.39	16.43	16.21
15	16.50	17.45	18.34	20.26	21.15	21.49	21.41	20.53	19.45	18.37	16.41	16.22
16	16.52	17.46	18.36	20.28	21.16	21.49	21.40	20.51	19.43	18.35	16.40	16.22
17	16.54	17.48	18.37	20.29	21.18	21.50	21.39	20.49	19.40	18.33	16.39	16.22
18	16.55	17.50	18.39	20.31	21.19	21.50	21.38	20.47	19.38	18.31	16.37	16.22
19	16.57	17.52	18.41	20.33	21.21	21.51	21.37	20.45	19.36	18.29	16.36	16.23
20	16.58	17.54	18.42	20.34	21.22	21.51	21.36	20.43	19.33	18.27	16.35	16.23
21	17.00	17.55	18.44	20.36	21.24	21.51	21.34	20.41	19.31	18.25	16.34	16.23
22	17.02	17.57	18.46	20.38	21.25	21.51	21.33	20.38	19.29	18.23	16.33	16.24
23	17.03	17.59	18.47	20.39	21.26	21.51	21.32	20.36	19.26	17.21	16.32	16.25
24	17.05	18.01	18.49	20.41	21.28	21.52	21.30	20.34	19.24	17.19	16.31	16.25
25	17.07	18.03	18.51	20.43	21.29	21.52	21.29	20.32	19.22	17.17	16.30	16.26
26	17.09	18.04	18.52	20.44	21.30	21.52	21.28	20.30	19.20	17.15	16.29	16.26
27	17.10	18.06	19.54	20.46	21.32	21.51	21.26	20.28	19.17	17.13	16.28	16.27
28	17.12	18.08	19.56	20.48	21.33	21.51	21.25	20.26	19.15	17.11	16.27	16.28
29	17.14		19.57	20.49	21.34	21.51	21.23	20.23	19.13	17.09	16.26	16.29
30	17.16		19.59	20.51	21.35	21.51	21.22	20.21	19.10	17.07	16.26	16.30
31	17.17		20.01		21.36		21.20	20.19		17.05		16.31

Note: The times above are when *headlamps* on vehicles must be switched on in the evenings. *Front and rear position lamps* must be used between sunset and sunrise. These times are in GMT, except between 01.00 on March 27 and 01.00 on October 23 when they are in BST (1 hour in advance of GMT). They are calculated for London (longitude 0°, latitude N.51°.5).